A

HUMMINGBIRD'S

AWAKENING

A HUMMINGBIRD'S
AWAKENING

RUSSO SHANIDZE

PALMETTO
PUBLISHING

Charleston, SC
www.PalmettoPublishing.com

A Hummingbird's Awakening
Copyright © 2021 by Russo Shanidze

First Edition

Printed in the United States

Hardcover ISBN: 978-1-63837-043-7
Paperback ISBN: 978-1-63837-044-4
eBook ISBN: 978-1-63837-045-1

A Hummingbird's Awakening is the memoir of a woman—the author—who has shared her story of a lovely childhood, struggling teenage years, and hardships of adulthood, as a single mother, in a provocative manner that could evoke an emotional upheaval. The book may elicit a wide range of feelings from gratefulness to sadness, fury, sympathy, deep anguish, and finally understanding. The book sends out a strong message to all those suffering silently in their lives on how a lost, broken soul can be led to the path of healing and forgiveness, making them a stronger and better version of themselves. In a world where it is extremely easy to give up on life, this story comes as a beacon of hope for thousands of people.

CONTENTS

PREFACE

Georgia is my birth country, where I took my first steps.
It taught me about traditions, cultures, and values,
and how to love Mother Earth.
At age sixteen, I fell in love, got married, and
left my sweet, loving nest.
This emotional tornado hurled me into adventures and
challenges
that took place in the marvelous country of Israel.
Imagine entering a new space with totally unfamiliar things;
it was extremely scary at first.
Besides all of those changes and struggles,
I was still only sixteen when I got pregnant
and then gave birth
to a beautiful boy who came into my life as a blessing;
he brought me so much strength.
I changed my residence from Israel to Turkey,
from Turkey to England, and then back to my homeland,
where I stayed for a while, worked, and used all of the
knowledge and skills

that I acquired from the various parts of this glamorous world.
In my mid-twenties, I met a charming artist
and I fell in love again.
I welcomed my second son, my little angel,
who was so difficult to raise; oh, it was intense!
I was always open to new wonders and opportunities
that were unfolding on my path,
I was curious and eager to learn.
I never stopped dreaming, growing, and evolving
no matter how many times I failed, got rejected, or even hurt.
I followed my heart's calling,
I was searching for more, perhaps for my purpose to be here,
but I didn't know what it was then.
I took a bold decision as a single mom and
immigrated to the United States.
Having two sons is a huge responsibility,
but it's even harder when their fathers, unfortunately,
couldn't be there for them.
There is so much more to say and share with you,
so I'll let you find out the rest.
One more thing which is so significant to tell you—
COVID-19 became a part of this book as well.
Thank you for reading my life story,
I am *so* thankful and *very* blessed!

1

HOW THE IDEA OF
A HUMMINGBIRD'S AWAKENING
WAS BORN

Los Angeles, California (2019)

I would have never started this book if *A Hummingbird's Nest*, my first novel, had not been written in the first place. There is even more; the title and idea of this book were born on November 13, 2019, when I had lunch with a unique lady named Cynthia Martin, Personal Freedom Activator, Spiritual Awakening & Mindset Coach,[1] whom I had met almost two years earlier to this meeting. At the end of our lunch, I gave Cynthia a signed copy of *A Hummingbird's Nest* and a poetry book of *A Hummingbird's Reminder*, which I wrote and published in 2019 too. Then I shared with her a dream that I had about hummingbirds. I had dreamed that my curly hair was like a nest. I put my hand into my hair and found three newborn hummingbirds. I got the first two hummingbirds out from my hair easily, but the last one was so tiny and fragile that it took me longer to get it out from my hair to feed. Once Cynthia heard my story, with a rousing voice, she told me, "Russo, your next book is going to be about what you've learned from your relationships and life experiences and call it 'A Hummingbird's Awakening'." After she said that, chills ran over my entire body for an instant. I felt like that this book, *A Hummingbird's Awakening*, was already born; it was there in the realm, but it was invisible to our eyes and I was ready to materialize and make this inspiring idea that was delivered by a beautiful messenger (Cynthia) visible to us all.

In 2018, I was working for one of the international media companies that was providing video reviews and online marketing services for consumers and small to medium enterprises and businesses in the United States. While I was doing this work, I had the opportunity to meet with Cynthia and offer her our video and online services for her work. This wasn't an accident or a coincidence. This meeting was meant to occur because when I met Cynthia, it had only been three months since I had broken up with my boyfriend, and I was in the process of grieving and going through an excruciating pain that was devilishly difficult to deal with. Deep inside, I was hurt and aching. Although other times I could hide my emotions, this time I wasn't as good an actress as I used to be, as I was unable to hide and compress the heartbreak and disappointment within myself, which I had always been capable of doing. This time, I had suffered enough and it finally awakened and widely opened me up. Eckhart Tolle, a spiritual teacher and author says, "You won't be able to surrender unless you're completely fed up with suffering, you've had enough suffering."[2] He is right. In other words, I finally surrendered and came to the moment of realization that I didn't want to be racked with pain anymore and I had a huge desire to heal myself; still, I didn't know how. Although I felt that I was on the path of awakening, where there was so much more, so much deeper and greater, I didn't know what it was. I was lost, confused, and searching for answers. I strongly believe that when you ask for help and guidance, this beautiful universe will assist and deliver the answers to you. "When you want something, all the universe conspires in helping you to achieve it"—Paulo Coelho, *The Alchemist*. For this reason, the universe brought me to Cynthia to find what I was searching to overcome during this extremely saddening time in my life. Along my journey, I've always practiced self-healing through positive thinking and prayers. Indeed, when I was hurt, I would act and pretend that everything was just fine. My *ego* kept telling me, "You are strong! Be positive, forget about it, and move on." However, this time it was different. I didn't want to be *positive*. I just wanted to be *me*, my *true self*. I wanted to *love myself* and wanted to know that I was *worthy* and that I *deserved happiness*. As I am writing this, tears are rolling down my face, though these are the tears of happiness!

But now, you all wonder, and you might be even thinking, who doesn't break up with their boyfriends, girlfriends, or partners? People get divorced after twenty, thirty, or forty years of marriages. Some people unexpectedly go through more horrendous and tragic experiences, like losing their loved ones, children, and family members. So, what's the big deal about breaking up with your boyfriend? I do agree! It wasn't about breaking up with my boyfriend, it was all about opening and speaking up and being able to say the truth—*the truth* that I had been suppressing and not facing for my entire life. The Persian poet Rumi said in one of his poems, "He said, 'How do you benefit from this life?' I said, 'By keeping true to myself.'" At last, I wanted to be true to myself.

Nevertheless, before I share more with you about this ineffable experience that ultimately liberated me from the imprisonment that I've lived for such a long time, I would like to go back and retrace my life from my adolescent years.

2

EARLY NINETIES - TBILISI, GEORGIA—
ONE OF THE FORMER
SOVIET REPUBLICS

It wouldn't be fair if I don't briefly introduce you to my native country where I spent my childhood—my birth country that is so dear and near to my heart.

I say the country of Georgia because people often get confused when they ask me about my originality and if my response is just Georgia, they automatically assume that I am talking about the beautiful southeastern Peach State of Georgia, although my accent in every respect is unlike those from that state, and that's what puzzles them.

Therefore, we have two Georgias in the world and one of them is the country (Georgian Sakartvelo) that is located at the crossroads where Eastern Europe meets Western Asia. It is bounded to the north by Russia, to the southeast by Azerbaijan, to the south by Armenia and Turkey, and to the west by the Black Sea.[3] Orthodox Christianity is the

main religion in Georgia. The roots of the Georgian people go deep in history and their cultural legacy is exotic and
unique, ancient and abundant. Hospitality and kindness are
engraved in Georgian culture. Georgian people believe that
"the guests are a gift from God," and they welcome them
with an open heart and offer them a delightful feast (supra).
Additionally, I've been asked many times if Georgia has its
own native language that is different from Russian or other Eastern European languages, so I would like to touch
upon the official language of Georgia, which is Georgian
(Kartvelian language). It is spoken by Georgians and has its
own script. Georgian is the most widespread and common of
the Kartvelian languages, a family that also contains Svan,
Mingrelian, and Laz, and this group of languages is not
known to be related to any others.[4]

I can write endlessly about this small, albeit immensely
rich, country with its remarkable history, authentic culture,
and traditions that also include food, wine, music, Georgian
folk dance, and much more. However, I'd like to focus on the
early years of the nineties, one of the most pivotal times of
my life and for the entire nation.

After being part of the Soviet Union for almost seventy
years, at last on April 9, 1991, Georgia declared its indepen-
dence and it was no longer one of the Soviet Union's republics, but rather a new country that has started to pursue a
western model of governance. On the one hand, the whole
nation was glorified and blessed for celebrating the democracy within the country. But on the other hand, the beginning
of the process was extremely destructive and catastrophic, as

almost every change is challenging and it can be chaotic and distressing at first.

The early nineties had been an agonizing time for everyone—there was a bloody civil war in Georgia, consisting of interethnic conflicts in the regions of Abkhazia (1992–1993) and South Ossetia (1988–1992), along with the brutal and murderous coup d'état from 1991 to 1993, against the first democratically elected president of Georgia, Zviad Gamsakhurdia, and his succeeding rebellion in an attempt to retake power.[5] In 1991, there were big demonstrations, violent clashes, and fatalities in the capital city of Tbilisi and a state of emergency was proclaimed in the city, where my family and friends lived. In the early nineties, I was a teenager and those striking days and years will never be erased from my memories. Although life seemed unbearable and miserable at that time—compounded by living for months without running water and power, witnessing citywide curfews, waiting in bread and water lines, using candle lights or kerosene lamps to do homework and kerosene stoves for cooking and even for heating the house—it's hard to say but I enjoyed my teenage years with my friends and family.

I grew up in a traditional Christian family that consisted of the two most loving parents, extraordinary grandparents, me, and my amazing brother (sometimes he drove me crazy and so did I him, as all siblings do to one another but, overall, my brother Lasha was very sweet, protective, and wonderful). Generosity and hospitality were the core values not only for my family but for every single Georgian family. For that reason, our house door was always open to everyone and food and drink were offered right away, especially *Georgian wine*. Even if you were a child, my grandfather would have still insisted that we taste a small piece of bread soaked in his homemade wine. Both of my grandfathers had such a deep connection with wine. The wine-making and -drinking traditions are indivisible from the country's identity. I recall, every time my paternal grandfather visited any of his friends or relatives, he used to take with him his homemade wine. He wouldn't drink any wine that wasn't exceptionally pure. There is something very unique about how my grandfathers, and not only them but all Georgians, love their wine, which is such an integral part of the culture and everyday life. My maternal grandfather used to make wine in a "Qvevri"— the large egg-shaped earthenware used for fermenting, storing, and aging the wine. ("Scholars say the word 'Qvevri' comes from 'kveuri,' which means 'that which is buried' or 'something dug deep in the ground'."[6]) All grandchildren, including me, used to help our grandfather with harvesting and then pressing the grapes. Afterwards, he would pour the juice, grape skins, pips, and stalks into a "Qvevri," which was then sealed. The tradition of making wine in a "Qvevri" is part of the Georgian cultural inheritance and identity. Everyone in my family, as well as all of our guests, used to enjoy my grandfathers' wine. To be honest with you, in my teenage years, I didn't like the taste of it; even when I became an adult, I wasn't fond of wine, though I still have my favorite, which is "Khvanchkara," a semi-sweet red wine. However, today I have a deep appreciation and awareness of a *good wine*, because I was exposed to it as a child.

Most people in Georgia grow up in friendly and tight-knit communities. During the nineties, when times were very demanding and tough, people bonded even more; shared food, water, candles, kerosene; helped each other within the neighborhood; showed their goodwill and compassion. Due to the fact that the entire country was going through these radical and distressing changes, parents were very concerned about their children's education and most importantly, the safety of their loved ones, especially for the boys because guns and firearms were easy to collect and get hold of at that time.

Consequently, my parents, especially my mom, who dedicated her entire life to my brother and me after twenty-five years of work as a music (piano) teacher, gave up her job when we became teenagers and was intensively involved in all of our activities. She was always there for my brother and me and was intensely checking on my brother every single day to make sure that he was safe and was coming straight home after school; that's how dangerous it was for the young boys to be outside in the streets. Almost every day, we used to hear about the death of a minor because the boys in those days used to get in trouble and they were shot. If it was not for my parents' unconditional love and undivided attention, care, and guidance, I, as well as my brother, would have been unable to take the courageous steps, choices, and life-altering changes that paved our future.

3

TEENAGE YEARS IN TBILISI, GEORGIA (1991–1993)

By nature, I was a very warm, high-spirited but meek, and curious teenager; on the other hand, I was also very earnest and stubborn when it came to dating boys. If anyone in school expressed their interest in me, with one frowning look and a very cold attitude, I would demolish their attractions towards me so rapidly that they didn't dare to say anything or even look at me when they saw me in school. This sounds a little mean, though I truly wasn't a mean girl. However, now I think that this was my way of showing to those boys that I was strong and tough and not vulnerable or naive. My close girlfriends knew me so well that they used to laugh a lot when I behaved that way. To be frank, I really didn't care about boys, love, or dating. I lived in my own imaginary world and I was totally focused on my schoolwork, friends, and other creative activities. One of my favorite pursuits that I was so passionate about and greatly admired was the

Georgian folk dance, a traditional dance of Georgia. I had been dancing from age five and pursued it to sixteen because I loved it so very much.

Let's talk about how everything changed when I turned fifteen. I had a wake-up call that took place a little bit later in my teen years, which means, at that age, I eventually noticed and became aware of my own self. I began looking in the mirror, which I had never cared for before, and started observing my own body—my face, my hair that was so curly, my eyebrows that were thick and rounded, my eyes were big and brown and my cheeks always looked pale. I had a little gap between my front teeth, which I never liked; therefore, I tried to hide it by not smiling or laughing, especially in front of boys. I was embarrassed and didn't want them to see it. Moreover, I started dressing up in front of the mirror, brushing my hair properly, and paying more attention to how I looked before I went to school or anywhere else. Finally, I became more conscious of my physical appearance and, surprisingly, made an effort to look nice or cute. In reality, that was a big transformation for me as a teenager.

Nevertheless, let me admit the truth, which I found out later in my life from my mom. Before this great change happened to me at age fifteen, my parents were the ones who were really, really worried about me. They were contemplating that I was almost fifteen and didn't care about my looks at all, didn't have any interest in flirting and, even worse, that I was still very immature and naïve. They thus thought that I would never ever date anyone or get married. Since marriage, family, and children are significantly important in the Georgian culture, it's obvious that my parents were concerned about me. Honestly, the only thing that I ever wanted when I had either short or long school breaks was to visit my maternal grandparents, who were the most loving, gracious, and generous people. My maternal grandfather was one of the most creative men I've ever known. As a little girl, I believed that he was a magician because there was nothing that he couldn't do. His hobbies were building, painting, and creating things, and he was extremely talented in every specialty such as plumbing, welding, carpentering, constructing, designing, etc. He was self-taught and built everything by himself—the house he lived in with my grandma, the pool with the fountains outside in the backyard, a billiard table, the sofas, armchairs, closets, and fireplaces. Surprisingly, he used to sew curtains, pillows, sofa covers, and table linens and make shoes by hand for my mother and her siblings, when they were little. Furthermore, prior to World War II, he was a working actor who performed in a few plays in the theaters along with other widely respected and recognized actors in Georgia. In addition to all of the above, he went to dental school when he already had his three children and became a dental technician who manufactured dental prosthetics. He had his own working office at his home and due to my curious nature, I had an opportunity to watch how he artistically created all of those crowns and dentures. Most of all, what I reminisce about my grandpa is that whatever he did, at all times, he put his heart and soul into it. Now, if my grandma was still with us (I believe she watches over me) she would be upset if I don't speak briefly of her. She actually was an outstanding cook; not only that, but she also had a beautiful and sweet voice when she played her lute and sang the songs she loved most. The best part of her playing the lute was when my grandpa joined her and recited his favorite poems with so much passion that, as a young girl, I was captivated by his distinctive voice and artistic command. Almost every night after dinner, my grandpa used to burn wood in the fireplace, create a cozy atmosphere for us (his grandchildren), and perform short scenes from his plays when he worked as a stage actor in his youth. He sang, danced, made jokes, and let us perform, sing, and dance with him too. He was an inspirational human being with a tender and caring soul, and his presence played a huge role during my childhood.

Moreover, they lived in a beautiful house with an enchanting garden that included a wide variety of majestic trees bearing delicious fruits: fig trees (my favorite), cherries, mulberries, apple, peach, pomegranate, pears, plums, persimmon . . . and other fruits like blackberries, strawberries, raspberries, assorted grapes, as well as all kinds of vegetables. Additionally, the wildflowers were decorating the backyard, next to the scented roses that were growing and blooming each year, and the most fragrant lilacs were making the garden especially spectacular. I was in love with those flowers and trees, with their essence, presence, and holiness. I indeed verbally expressed to them how beautiful and magnificent they were and sometimes sang some songs to them if I was alone; I felt that they heard me. I believe what I sensed then, as a young girl, was that when you give your attention and love to flowers and trees, they recognize their liveness through your presence, and they give you back the scent of love. The love that I've derived from the divine nature since my childhood has stayed within me forever. Hence, I would like to share with you the following poem that I recently wrote about the wildflowers—it is a reminder of how everything on earth is unique, exquisitely interconnected, and has its purpose. It's a blessing to be living *here*.

The Wildflowers' Whisper

The wildflowers whisper in the garden—
"What's the point for us to grow here
When the most fragrant roses are blooming
So near?
They are crowned the queens of the flowers
And they derive all of the attention every day
For hours.
The sun clasps its rays around their thorns
And kisses the roses' buds and petals
With so much love and warmth.
What about us?
No one knows how we feel all day—
We have emotions, passion, and
We love to dance and sway."
The one little rose in the garden heard
The wildflowers' grievances and complaints.

It stood still and silent.
Then it turned towards them
And spoke in a sweet and humble way—
"Your presence makes this garden so precious and whole,
Your free spirit and resilience encourage us all.
Your bright, colored dresses decorate the earth,
You make us feel alive;
We are all so blessed."

Needless to say, visiting my grandparents was a big celebration for me; they both were remarkable, and I was blessed for having them in my life. Besides, each time, I was looking forward to seeing my neighbors, six kids from age three to thirteen, and my two little cousins at age four and five. I was the oldest and unfailingly I was very caring, nurturing, and considerate, so the parents of those kids, along with my grandparents, trusted me fully with their little ones. I was always happy to take care of my little cousins. I was vigilant where they were concerned and was attentive to our neighbors' kids as well. So, among all of the fun games we played and various creative things we did together, one of the most favorite activities that I enjoyed was climbing all kinds of trees, especially fruit trees like mulberries, figs, and cherries. While I was staying at my grandparents' house during the summer break, I remember sitting on a mulberry tree almost every day, literally for hours, chatting with the neighbors' kids, and plucking a handful of black mulberries off the tree and stuffing them into my mouth. They were so juicy and rich and filled me up so much that I never wished to eat anything else afterwards. I was a very picky eater—not only then, I'm still fussy—though I enormously enjoyed eating those fresh fruits from various trees. I think having that kind of magical childhood that was filled with so much love, warmth, and beauty, in those days, was more appealing and attractive to me than boys.

4

LOVE CONFESSION
TBILISI, GEORGIA (1992)

The winter is very cold in Georgia. We mostly stayed indoors for any gatherings or events, not only because of the cold climate but also because of an unsafe and stressful social, economic, and political situation in the country. I was almost fifteen and a half and had a short school break for winter. One of the evenings during the holidays, a couple of my friends and I were joining a party at my brother's friend's apartment. The party was small and cheerful, yet it was one of the most shocking nights for me because my brother's best friend, named Erekle, almost seventeen years old, finally confessed his feelings for me and his plans for us together in a very decisive and romantic way. I say *finally* because he kept this secret from me for five months, although everyone knew about it—all of his friends, his family, my brother, and even my own mother but me, which shows how naive I was—I had no clue. This whole incident for me was so unexpected and sudden, especially when he revealed his feelings for me. Plus, he said with confidence that one day he wanted me to become the mother of his children. I was totally blown away and speechless. I don't recall anything I said that evening, though what I remember so clearly is that my face and cheeks were flushed. I was blushing the entire time while he was talking so passionately. Not to mention, I was little scared and embarrassed, but I still liked hearing his loving and sweet words; he was absolutely adorable. Actually, he was nervous too, because while he was professing his feelings for me, he was holding a box of wooden matches and kept taking out each match from the box, one by one, and kept breaking them nonstop. After a long love confession, a small coffee table was full of completely destroyed matches and the box was empty. He looked at the matches, then at me, and at that instant, we both burst out laughing. It was one of those moments that you can never forget. In fact, after the party, it was my first night as a teenager that I was unable to sleep because of this overwhelming revelation, which I barely believed, and it kept me up the entire night.

Erekle was my brother's very dear friend, one of his best friends, and they went to the same school. In reality, my brother moved to Erekle's school and spent his junior and senior years in the same school with him. They were the best buddies and loved each other very much. We all knew Erekle since he was thirteen because that's when my brother and he started hanging out together and established their friendship, plus he was our neighbor. Once my brother moved to his school, every single morning, he would walk to our house

and holler my brother's name so loudly that the whole neighborhood was awakened at the same time. Everyone knew
and loved him so much that no one really cared to say anything about his thunderous and ringing voice. He was our
neighbors' morning alarm. After school, my brother's friends
used to hang out in our house because it was so risky and
hazardous for young boys to be outside in those days; parents preferred to keep their children in one of the other parents' houses. As a result, they loved to come to our place very
often. My mom was home almost on all occasions and she
would make the most delicious Georgian traditional cheese
bread (Khachapuri) and, of course, other things too; none-
theless, the cheese bread was everyone's favorite.

As far as Erekle is concerned, he was a tall, well-built
guy with rich chocolate hair; his eyes were dark brown with
thick eyelashes; his skin was tanned, and he had the cutest
smile with dimples on his cheeks. At school, he was one of
the most popular boys who used to play the guitar so beautifully, had the most charming voice, and danced very well.
Many girls were in love with him at school and, therefore, he
used to date and even had a longtime girlfriend (according
to my knowledge). Since my brother's friends were frequent
visitors to my family, I knew them all very well and liked and
respected them, and I only considered them as my brother's
pals. I never had any other interests in them. And even that
day, when Erekle revealed his feelings to me, I thought that
he had a girlfriend. Quite often, when he spent an evening
with us, he would ask my mom and me to sing together. He
particularly loved one song that I used to play on the piano,

and I assumed it reminded him of his partner. I certainly was a very childish and inexperienced girl who certainly lived in her own visionary world. I used to tell my mom, "He must be truly in love with his girlfriend." By the way, while my mom was an amazing piano teacher, she had an incredibly beautiful voice as well. She taught me how to sing and play the piano, I was OK in both. I would surely *not* sing in public with my type of voice, but I felt comfortable singing among my family and friends, especially when my mom and I sang duets together.

When I found out that Erekle, such an incredibly cute and charming boy, was in love with me, I kept questioning myself and reflecting on this whole thing because I really wasn't a popular girl in school. I never made any romantic advances towards boys. Primarily, I was reserved and serious when I was around guys. Therefore, I was curious to know what feature drew Erekle towards me. In truth, my main interest was to dance, to hang out with my girlfriends after school and later in the evening, and to chat with them over the corded phone until my paternal grandfather interrupted our "deep conversation" with his repetitive "alo . . . alo . . . alo" (which means hello) from another corded phone in his room. He would then blow air into the phone endlessly, thinking that by doing so he could clear the line. Hence, my only option was to hang up on whomever I was talking to. When we had school events, contests, or performances, my role was to recite the poems written by the renowned Georgian poets. I've had so much admiration for poetry since childhood. I've been collecting poetry books and I have loved every poet for their distinctive writing and style, hence never stopped learning poems along with writing my own too.

Galaktion Tabidze, one of the most recognizable Georgian poets of the early twentieth century, was my favorite poet and I knew almost all of his well-known poems. However, "The Moon over Mtatsminda" was the one, among other breathtaking poems, that I used to recite a lot when I performed.

> *My eyes have never seen the moon so lovely as tonight;*
> *In silence wrapped it is the breathless music of the night.*
> *Moonbeams embroider shadows with fine thread of silver light;*
> *O, eyes have never seen the sky so lovely as tonight!*[7]
> —Galaktion Tabidze

I look back on those days when Erekle used to come to our house and ask me to either play the piano or recite some of the poems that I knew. He would be so engaged in the poems and loved to listen to me and then he would play the guitar and sing some songs with his endearing voice. Apparently, that's what he found appealing and interesting in me; perhaps he saw who I really was then.

5

Erekle's and my relationship had the sweetest and most daz-
zling start. Nearly every single day after his college classes, he would spend the rest of the day with us; he loved my
family very much and they loved him too. Every time when
I needed to be picked up either from my dancing classes or
from tutors, Erekle replaced my mom and he was the one
who used to escort me everywhere and protect me all the
time. He was a true gentleman. Therefore, he was granted
trust from my parents. I had invariably avoided befriending
boys before Erekle and I became a couple. As a result, in the
beginning of our relationship, I felt a bit awkward to sit close
to him or even touch him. His experience was even worse,
which I found out later from him. He didn't know how to
come close to me and hold my hand, especially when we
walked together; he was terribly nervous and frightened. He
felt that there was an iceberg between us and he needed to

break through it in order to come nearer to me, but fear was holding him back.

One evening, when Erekle came to pick me up from my dancing class, it was freezing cold outside. Everything was dark and there was no power in the city. The streets and sidewalks were slippery. The city looked neglected. As we were walking side by side, I could sense that his entire attention was on me to make sure that I didn't fall and hurt myself, yet he was very shy to hold my hand. Unquestionably, girls are much more courageous in teenage years, so I took a bold step and broke the iceberg that was keeping us apart. I took my hand out of my warm winter coat, quickly grabbed his hand, held it tight, and continued walking. There was a short silence, and then with full, thrilling energy, he started bouncing like a little boy. At once, he pressed his palm against mine so strongly that I thought he would never let it go.

Starting a relationship at a young age has its own advantages: you grow, learn, and experience things together; you are more open, truthful, and vulnerable with each other; you don't carry any baggage from the past, as well. And lastly, you take more risks in life, without having the fear of failing or anticipating any negative outcome. Mostly, you live in the moment, day by day; well, that's how I lived. I was in love and enjoyed every bit I spent with my sweetheart. Of course, I can't deny that in your youth, you do so many crazy things too, but that's part of a teenager's life.

Erekle knew the depth of my affection and passion for nature, flowers, and poetry, and he consistently attempted to surprise me by bringing the most vibrant and perfumed flowers accompanied by a small poem or a love letter every time he came to see me—he never missed once. Even those days when he wasn't able to come, or was out of town, he would send someone with a bouquet of roses as a reminder of his intense feelings and devotion. I still have some of his love notes and poems written in my childhood diary and when I read them now, I'm convinced that he was frightfully deep and poignant. I'd like to share with you one of his short poems that he wrote in my diary and dedicated to me when he was just seventeen. I don't know if my translation from Georgian to English does his poem justice, but these are his words:

> *Keep, my beloved, this love note*
> *As a memory of our sweet days*
> *And if we ever are destined to fall apart,*
> *This poem will ignite the sparkle in your heart.*
> *Forever Yours,*
> —Erekle

6

THE METRO (THE SUBWAY)
TBILISI, GEORGIA (1993)

One of my close friends lived a little further from the city and it was her birthday celebration at her house. Erekle and I were invited along with one of Erekle's best friends, George. It was late, perhaps 11 p.m., when we left the party, and we took the metro (the subway) to go home. The vivid evocation of that night yet remains within me. The metro car that we entered into was empty, it was just the three of us. As soon as we sat down, in a few seconds, a group of gangsters (young adults) from another wagon (train car) entered our car. They were armed and were dressed in black winter jackets that covered their necks up to their chins and their hats concealed their foreheads completely; they looked intensely terrifying. I quickly glimpsed at them and then faintly smiled at Erekle. He sensed my fears and grabbed my hand and a fleeting silence arose until one of the gang members approached us with a nasty look and, in a raspy voice, he asked

Erekle, "Hey, bro, have you got a spare cigarette?" Erekle was holding a half-smoked cigarette (a butt) in his hand; that was the only one left and he kept it because he didn't want to smoke inside the train and was waiting to get out. Hence, he spontaneously offered his last cig (square) to the guy. In the meantime, George was sitting across from us quietly and still. He was just observing everything. I recall that he was carrying a small revolver in his outside coat pocket. The other gang members (around four or five men) were soundlessly standing at a little distance from us. Erekle's offer didn't satisfy that creepy-looking guy. He didn't say a word; however, his grim expression was more than enough to know that he was looking for trouble. They all were heavily armed and hostile, and we were the only ones in our wagon. It was fairly easy for them to do whatever they desired. The next stop was arriving, the train was slowing down. Erekle gently rose from his seat and respectfully asked that bully guy to get off the train and talk outside. Meanwhile, he kept holding my hand tight. It's apparent that anyone would have been petrified in my situation, and I was. But deep inside, I was confident that everything was going to be fine. The one thing though I was certain about was that if I said a word to that ferocious young man (of course, not in a bad way but in a nice way) and his reaction to my words turned offensive and ugly, somebody that night would have gotten killed, if not all of us. In those days in Georgia, many young guys (mostly teenagers) died while protecting their girlfriends. They were ready to face and endure danger or pain for their loved ones, and that's how they proved their loyalty and love. It seems crazy and unfortunate, but that's the truth. However, the only thought that I had in my head was to leave this group of criminals peacefully and get home safe. I was worried about my mom more than anything, because I knew if something happened to me, she would not survive. Erekle followed the same tactic; he remained humble the entire time. His biggest goal that night was to bring me home to my parents safe. He naturally considered himself responsible for my well-being when we were together. Consequently, when we got off the train, Erekle let go of my hand, got close to the same gang member, and spoke to him in a low voice so that no one could hear. I didn't know what was happening, though I recollect the moment when that wild-looking guy and I made an eye contact after Erekle murmured and then he surprisingly dismissed only Erekle and me, yet George stayed with them.

I asked Erekle, "Why did he let us go? What did you tell him?"

His response was, "I told him that you are my fiancé, we are getting married soon, and I want to make sure you get home safe."

I wasn't expecting him to say that; we were not engaged, though it was really sweet of him to say that, and his behavior was modest and amicable, which actually worked. I couldn't believe that we ultimately got out from the metro unhurt.

I was skipping and hopping with excitement, but then I asked Erekle, "What about George? Why didn't he come with us?"

He replied, "Don't worry about him; he will be fine."

Thankfully, everyone survived from that horrifying experience, George got home unharmed as well. That criminal group sought to bully and intimidate someone that night and they endeavored to challenge Erekle with a spiteful approach. In most cases, the outcome would have been dreadful. But, on the contrary, it ended without violence. They didn't get a vengeful reaction from us as they might have expected, which would have instigated a fight; instead they were treated in a benign manner. Gary Zukav, author of *The Seat of the Soul*, said, "For every action there is an equal and opposite reaction. You receive from the world what you give to the world." I believe if we treat each other with kindness and compassion, which are not weaknesses but quite the opposite, the world would be a better, safer, and more peaceful place to live.

7

PREPARING FOR THE UNIVERSITY
AND
AN UNEXPECTED PROPOSAL
TBILISI, GEORGIA (1993)

It was my last year in high school and I was intensely preparing myself for the university. I don't know whether it was
mine or my parents' or maternal grandparents' ambition
for me to become a dentist but it was crystal clear that my
grandparents wished that I had the same profession as them.
They were hopeful to have one of their grandchildren continue their occupation so that they could pass on their assets
that included all of their dental equipment and belongings.
As a matter of fact, one of their grandchildren did become a
successful dentist—my cousin, Nino. She was an outstanding
"A" student and was brilliant in math, science, and chemistry, unlike me. Even though I was diligent and studious
and tried so hard to study math and chemistry, I didn't seem
to have a firm grasp over them. It wasn't making sense; I

struggled, but I still desired to be a dentist and I don't know why. Perhaps, I just wanted to please my family, make them proud of me. To be frank, it wasn't only that; I aspired to be a dentist, to wear a white coat—the same way as my grandma—and to have a cozy, private dental office, where everything was immaculate. As a matter of fact, my grandparents didn't have an assistant at home, where they had their private dental workplace, and every time I visited them, I was eager to help. My main duty was to clean the office and disinfect the various dental tools. My grandmother was constantly checking on me to make sure that I was following all the rules. She even taught me how to give a shot, not in the mouth of course, I was too young for that, but on the backside. And according to her, I was a very good student. I definitely was a very organized, neat, cautious, committed, and patient girl, except for two of the most prime components that were missing—I was terrible at math and chemistry. It's an irony that I was persistently pursuing becoming a dentist, because I didn't want to disappoint my family.

In the meantime, while studying so hard, my attention was on Erekle as well. His family was highly concerned about his well-being in Georgia, like every other parent. Erekle came from a significantly affluent family. His mother was an optometrist, whereas his father worked for the Georgian government; he was a member of parliament. But prior to that, Erekle's father had a lucrative business in the food processing industry. Consequently, Erekle's family was financially capable of sending their son overseas for his protection. Therefore, Teymuraz, Erekle's father, initiated a proposition with one of his business partners who lived in Ashdod, Israel, and with whom he was in the process of constructing and establishing a new enterprise that was located in Israel. Erekle's father wished his son to work and eventually manage and run the company that he was building with his business partners. It was quite a great strategy developed by Erekle's family. They sought to keep their son away from the perils in Georgia and were desperate to get him out of the disruptive city of Tbilisi.

❦

Time was running out; it was already mid-spring 1993. Erekle was turning eighteen and his parents were ready to move forward with this life-changing plan for their son. Nevertheless, Erekle was utterly against his parents' arrangements and intent. He refused to move to Israel without me. So, out of the blue, in May, Erekle proposed and asked me to marry him and move to Israel with him. That news stunned everyone, including me. I was getting ready for medical school and suddenly, so unexpectedly, my boyfriend proposed to me. He was willing to move to Israel only if I went with him. Otherwise, he wasn't going anywhere. He was worried and concerned about leaving me in Tbilisi. He kept saying that he didn't want to lose me and if he moved to Israel by himself, he might because I could meet someone else while he was gone and that would break his heart. Although I tried to assure him that the love I had for him was so strong and real that I wouldn't date or go out with anybody, and I would wait for him as long as it took, no matter what I said, he listened

31

neither to me nor anyone else. At some point, he got so frustrated about this issue of him moving to Israel by himself that once while we were talking in my living room, just the two of us, he took a sharp knife out of his pocket and cut his hand in front of me so deeply that the blood spurted over the floor, and instead of getting up and helping him to prevent bleeding, I took the same knife and cut my hand at the same spot where he had his wound. The only difference was that his cut was really drastic and severe unlike mine. Everything happened so instantly that we both were astounded by our behavior, so much so that for a few seconds, we were standing in the middle of the living room and watching each other's blood gushing out in a sudden and forceful stream. We were two crazy teenagers! Then I grabbed his hand quickly and took him to the bathroom, where we washed ourselves. I took care of him and myself properly and, as might be expected, we both cleaned the floor so no one would notice our insane mess. Later, we ended up in the hospital, since his cut was really bad and needed a few stitches.

Due to this bloody incident, I knew for sure that Erekle would not go or move anywhere unless I joined him. By hurting himself physically that day, he demonstrated his passionate love towards me. He expressed that being without me would be as painful as that wound, even worse. As far as I was concerned, I don't know what the purpose was for me to injure myself; that happened so fast, me holding a knife and cutting my hand! That was appalling. Now, while I am writing this, I'm asking that young Russo in me this question that I never asked before, because I never had a desire to ruminate about this unpleasant episode that occurred in my life. *Why did I hurt myself?* And the answer is that the young Russo in me wished to verify her love and loyalty to Erekle, by showing him that if he could cut, she could do it too. I believe, that was also a way of displaying my fortitude to him.

Nevertheless, the most critical, surprising, yet exciting outcome of this wild event was that I accepted Erekle's proposal and decided to marry him. I loved Erekle and didn't want to let him down. I was ready to move to Israel with him and that meant I was willing to give up pursuing dentistry in Georgia. I was also ready to leave my family, friends, and everything behind and step into an unknown space and allow myself to see the potential for a new world and new possibilities. As Jean Houston describes in her inspiring book *The Wizard of Us: Transformational Lessons from Oz,* "The fork in the road can be frightening—for the hero doesn't know what lies ahead."[8] For me, that fork in the road represented a huge opportunity and freedom. It was indeed a little scary, still very thrilling and encouraging. I was just sixteen and what I can discern now is that I was eager to encounter a vital life change that was coming from the curiosity and inquisitiveness that I had for the mysterious and unfamiliar society. I had a yearning for something more, for an adventure, and for seeing what life was going to unfold along my journey. For that reason, the marriage proposal at that time was as if a tornado hit me, not the house, and hurled me into trials and challenges in a new world for which I had no preparation at all, yet complete faith in my ability to embark on this quest. Erekle, however, came into my life as a catalyst to get that change happening and to transform my life on a deep level. Let's pause here and go back and find out how my parents faced this abrupt frightful news that came as a bombshell. At the same time, I would like to discuss more about the early marriages that were frequently occurring in the nineties in Georgia.

❧

After the breakup of the Soviet Union, when unemployment, socioeconomic instability, and hardships were prevailing and the country was going through drastic changes, the schools were periodically closed because of the insecurity and danger in the city. Education thus significantly lost its value. Despite that fact, the young generation, like myself, was determined and committed to pursue their education, and concurrently they were willing to get married and raise a family. The child marriage rates grew dramatically in the nineties for several reasons. But one of the major causes was that the Georgian society put high value on virginity, and in order to have intimate relationships with partners and to avoid social disapproval or stigma, marriage was the only choice to legalize intimacy (couples could legally get married at age sixteen in the nineties in Georgia). Regardless of the age, many girls and boys used to get married from the ages of fourteen to eighteen and it frankly became uncontrollable by parents. For those who were younger than sixteen, the marriages were performed by the church and were not officially registered; therefore, the rate of cohabitation was climbing fast as well. What I imply by the word *uncontrollable* is that if the parents rejected the marriage of their child, they would still elope from their home and marry their chosen partner secretly. In reality, there were a large number of runaway couples that got married covertly, and after a period of time, most parents consented to the marriages, except for some that were in absolute denial. In addition to this, not only did minor marriages increase in the nineties, but the childbirth rates were rising considerably.

Regarding my parents, they were both thunderstruck by this revelation, especially my father, who was overwhelmingly stressed about this news, and he kept telling my mom that I was too young and not ready at all for such an enormous change in my life. My mom agreed with my dad and they both tried to persuade me to alter my plans with Erekle. The irony was that a year and a half prior to this announcement, my parents were worried tremendously about me that I would never date or get married, and then shortly after, they were exceedingly anxious and distressed about me accepting a marriage proposal and getting married so young. Naturally, they both loved me unconditionally and were worried about me. They didn't want me to get hurt due to this swift decision. I recall that day so well when my father told me these words in an earnest and wholehearted manner: "Honey, you are very young; you are a little girl who needs so much to learn, grow, and evolve, you've got your entire life ahead of you. Marriage is not a fairy tale; it comes with a huge responsibility and commitment and neither you nor Erekle is prepared for this. Even though we all love Erekle so much, getting married at this age will not last a long time, maybe around one or two years, and then you will come back to us and say, 'I can't live with him anymore, it's over.'" He was very brief and articulate. He sensed that I didn't want to hear any of that, albeit I listened to him quietly with so much respect. He wasn't angry at me, though he was very disappointed and sad. I've never thought about that day until now, about his sorrowful eyes and low-spirited face when he was looking at me; I broke his heart at that time, and by writing this now, it breaks mine because I am a mother of two wonderful sons whom I love unconditionally too, and now I know for sure how he felt as a father and parent.

Unfortunately, no one was able to change our minds. Erekle and I were persistent about getting married and moving to Israel together, where we both were willing to go back to school. First we wished to learn the language, Hebrew, and then we had a desire to continue our education on a higher level. Erekle's parents were very supportive and optimistic about this whole thing. They came to see my parents and made an effort to assure my mom and dad that we both would be totally fine and safe in Israel. They would take care of us in every possible way, which included school and college tuition, housekeeping, medical bills, insurance, etc. They promised my parents that they would provide and arrange everything for Erekle and me so that we would be only focusing on our school and education. Needless to say, they were very empathetic and understandable towards my parents, knowing how overwhelmingly difficult and emotional this decision was for them.

The only reason my parents accepted this course of action was for our well-being and security. They knew if we moved to Israel, it would have benefited us in many different ways. First and foremost, we would have been safe and able to get a decent education, which is every parent's dream for his or her child. They thought that this was a rare opportunity that doesn't arise all the time and decided to pursue it with us together.

8

THE MOMENT OF MY WEDDING DAY THAT I REMEMBER VIVIDLY TBILISI, GEORGIA (JULY 1993)

Historically, a Georgian wedding is a glamorous, entertaining, and rich holiday with the ritual of all authentic traditions and customs. One of the most central parts of the wedding is the abundance of invited guests. In truth, the number of guests occasionally could exceed several hundreds because you don't want to hurt anyone's feelings, and each side of the families invite almost every close or distant relative or family friends. Therefore, the Georgian weddings are known to be enormous with a wide variety of traditional, exotic dishes and Georgian wine, folk singing and dancing, beautiful toasts, and vibrant Georgian music. Additionally, one of the traditions that is prevalent in Georgia is for the groom and his best men to pick up the bride at her house on the wedding day, where the groomsmen are welcomed by the head of the family, the bridesmaids, and close family friends with a little reception. The hosts and guests drink a glass of wine and wish the bride and groom joy and happiness. Afterwards, everyone drives together to the ceremony, whereas, by the Catholic tradition, it's bad luck for the groom to see the bride in her wedding dress prior to the ceremony.

Erekle's and my "big day" was orchestrated marvelously by our parents together. Both parties took care of everything, every single detail, which didn't bother me at all. Frankly, I was content that I didn't need to organize, design, or do anything. I was very confident that everything was going to be just perfect. I strongly believed that I was marrying my prince, who was going to rescue me and take me to a mysterious land where I envisioned that our *happily ever after* would begin.

Our wedding day took place in the first week of July 1993. It emerged overly fast, in fact, everything was ideally prepared and assembled in less than two months. Both of our parents tried to expedite everything because they wanted us to leave the city as soon as possible for our safety and well-being. I hardly reminisce about that short period of time of the whole planning process, obviously it's because I didn't participate in it. I mostly spent all of my days and time with Erekle and friends. However, what I remember so vividly about my special day is that I was standing in front of the mirror, already dressed up in a graceful, feminine wedding gown with an updo hairstyle. No one was in the room with me—I was alone, doing the final touchups before Erekle and groomsmen arrived. All of a sudden, I paused, became very still, looked at myself in the mirror, and then in a few seconds

I asked these questions to my own reflection: *Is this my wedding day? Is this really what I want?* I don't know what provoked me to ask these questions at first, and I recall so vividly that I was asking those questions to my own reflection in the mirror, in a way that it seemed like I was talking to another person. I didn't know what it was then, and I can't give you an exact answer even now; however, I believe that it was a fleeting moment of consciousness that arose in an instant and then it quickly disappeared once my mom entered the room and my mind took over. As a matter of fact, while writing this chapter, I've contemplated the brief scene of that day a lot and it was neither about the actual wedding ceremony nor about Erekle. It was all about *me*. So, during that time, as I was looking at myself in the mirror, I became fully aware and that's when I heard my inner voice trying to communicate with me by posing those questions. It beckoned me with the truth, which I instantly muted and completely ignored because I was too young and not ready to hear or face the truth yet and was instead looking forward to embarking on a new life-changing adventure no matter how daring, demanding, or scary it was going to be. Regardless of my age, I was determined to step out from the comfort zone that my family created for me, leave the known world behind, and set forth into an unknown. Hence, I believe my early marriage was the call for a fundamental change in my own life, which I accepted with courage and perseverance.

9

ASHDOD, ISRAEL (JULY 1993)

Two weeks after the wedding, Erekle and I ended up in Israel, where our new challenging journey commenced. I recall now that the beginning of that journey was similar to the beloved story of Dorothy from *The Wonderful Wizard of Oz* by L. Frank Baum. I felt as if the wind howled vigorously around me and, all of a sudden, a cyclone threw my husband and me into the historical and beautiful city of Ashdod.

Ashdod is the busiest, sixth-largest city, and the largest port in Israel. It is located on the Mediterranean coast of Israel and is situated between Tel Aviv to the north thirty-two kilometers away, Ashkelon to the south twenty kilometers away, and Jerusalem fifty-three kilometers to the east.[9] It's been more than two decades since I've lived in Ashdod and when I think back to that city, I recall that it was a neat, lovely, and safe place to live with plenty of shops, outdoor cafes, great restaurants, a friendly neighborhood, and beautiful long beaches. The city was in a development mode and the population was increasing drastically. In the nineties, immigrants from the former Soviet Union and Ethiopia were main contributors to the extensive population growth.

The apartment building that we lived in was located in the center of the city. Everything was within walking distance: the grocery stores, shops, cafes, the beach and, most importantly, our Hebrew learning school called *ulpan*. An ulpan is a school for the intensive study of Hebrew; the word "ulpan" itself is a Hebrew word, which means "teaching" or "instruction." In an ulpan, Hebrew learning is available at six main levels, starting from complete beginner (Aleph) to upper advanced (Vav). I couldn't wait to begin the school and learn a new language. I've always been thirsty to learn new things throughout my life.

Now, let's begin from the first day of our arrival in Ashdod and how excited I was to see our new apartment, where Erekle and I were going to establish our new home. Our three-bedroom apartment was already set up and ready for us. It was located on the fifth floor in a nice residential building. After our tiring flight, as soon as we opened the door and entered into the hallway, I had a shocking moment that could never be erased from my memory. It was late evening and the whole apartment inside was filthy! The old mattresses were all piled up in the middle of the living room—a dirty and unaired room—and they were covered by thick dust. On top of that, there were dead cockroaches lying on the floor almost everywhere in the house. The smell inside was awful and the apartment was hardly furnished. In the living room, there was only an old, damaged wooden dining table standing in the corner with six wooden chairs with wobbly legs, and the two of those chairs' backs were broken, so we had to be very careful to sit on them. The kitchen was equipped with just a few cabinets, a stained, dirty sink, and an old refrigerator with greasy shelves and drawers. There was no stove in the kitchen—we had to purchase one. Next to the kitchen, there was a tiny little laundry room that looked abandoned with an ugly and uninviting washing machine. The two smaller bedrooms in the apartment were totally empty with dead bugs on the floor, and the master bedroom was equipped with only a queen-size bed frame and headboard; that's all. I prefer not to describe the bathrooms, because by now you already have a clear picture of what our first place together looked like.

For a short period of time, we were standing silently; we were both too stunned to say anything. Afterwards, even though I was unable to observe my shocking face, I could still witness Erekle's disgraceful reaction to all of this. Honestly, I wasn't angry or wanting to blame anyone; this whole thing was so unexpected that I didn't know how to calm the tension at first. The only thing I knew was that we weren't in Georgia with our families anymore, we chose this path together, and we needed to deal with that by ourselves. I also knew that no one would've come and cleaned our apartment that night. So instead of resisting it, I accepted it as it was. As a child, whenever I used to visit my maternal grandparents, the first thing that I loved to do was to clean the entire house. No one has ever asked me to do any cleaning. It was always my choice and I tremendously enjoyed doing it—sweeping the floors, washing windows, stairs, bathrooms, and even ironing my little cousins' clothes. These two incredibly sweet boys, were my best friends, helpers, and teammates; they used to do everything, whatever I asked. I loved them unconditionally and they loved me back.

Consequently, after a long inspection of the entire place, I realized that night that I needed to use my house-cleaning skills, find any cleaning tools and supplies that were available in the apartment, and begin the home makeover with my husband. Erekle had lots of strength and energy (he was almost six feet two, well-built, muscular, whereas I was five feet five, between one hundred six to one hundred nine pounds). I was small, but still very energetic and healthy. Pretty much all night we stayed up and scrubbed, washed, cleaned, sterilized, and aired out the whole apartment. We truly did an amazing job, though the next day we were both dead tired and spent all day in bed but we were delighted that we didn't have those frightful dead cockroaches in our place any longer.

Starting a new life in another country—without family and friends, with a different language, unfamiliar traditions, and culture—was exceedingly challenging and difficult for both of us. Fortunately, in the beginning, my father-in-law's business partner and his lovely wife graciously helped us to enroll in an ulpan. They also found a private medical clinic for us, in case we needed a doctor for anything. We were grateful that we had them in the same town in case of emergency or if we ever had any questions. On all occasions, they were very supportive, helpful, and kind.

This complete and rapid change noticeably affected Erekle's personality. He was becoming very uncomfortable, impatient, and even aggressive about things. For example, at the beginning, when we moved into our apartment in Ashdod, we needed to set up utilities by physically going to the utility service providers' offices to schedule installation dates and times. This included cable, phone, water, gas, electricity, and waste disposal. Also, we needed to do grocery shopping and run other errands together. So, every time we went to those places, he never wanted to speak to anyone. He used to push me first everywhere we went and sometimes he would yell at me if I didn't understand something or if I asked the same question again for clarity. Everything for me was so new and unrelated that I needed to ask as many questions as possible to understand and learn. Luckily, in Israel, the Russian language was spoken by a large proportion of the population, mostly by immigrants who came from the former Soviet Union in the early nineties. Even though we didn't know Hebrew yet, we had an opportunity to speak in Russian, which was our second language in Georgia and we both spoke it well. In spite of that, Erekle wasn't comfortable interacting with others and did not even attempt to become more sociable and friendly; on the contrary, he was introverted and withdrawn. Although I disliked his behavior, especially when he yelled at me in public, and politely told him many times to not raise his voice at me anywhere because it was humiliating and disdainful, I still chose to be tolerant and patient towards him, because I sensed that he was stressed, self-conscious, and homesick. He never conveyed any of those feelings to me then, for the reason that he didn't want me to think that he was weak and incapable of dealing with those demanding situations and change. But I knew that's how he felt because I felt the same. I was missing my family, especially my mom, her cooking, her care and love. I was scared too. I didn't know how to cook and how to handle all of these enormous responsibilities.

In retrospect, we both stayed hopeful and constructive and decided to focus on our schoolwork and learn Hebrew fluently so we could pursue a higher education, which was our major goal. Every single morning, we would get up early, prepare our breakfast, and walk together to our ulpan. We had a wonderful class with a diversity of immigrants from all over the world, of all ages, and everyone was so friendly and helpful. That was an extraordinary experience for me, after my high school, to have this incredible opportunity of being among all of those fabulous people and learning a new language. I have to admit the truth. During his final years of high school, Erekle was a lazy, easily distracted, and unmotivated student in Georgia. The only thing he loved to do was to play guitar, sing, and hang out with his friends. I couldn't blame him because the whole educational system within the country was terribly affected by the political and social unrest. As a result, in the nineties, so many teenagers, particularly boys, lost their interest in studying. Surprisingly, in Israel, Erekle turned into a committed and diligent student. His hard work and tenacity were remarkable. In fact, he witnessed how much time I was putting into my homework and how committed and driven I was, so he desired to do the same. We both motivated each other and did extremely well in ulpan, though I must give huge credit to our Hebrew teacher. She was one of the best teachers I've ever had in my life. She didn't speak any other languages but Hebrew, and everyone in our class was just a beginner. Still, at the end of the day, we all understood everything she taught us. She was an excellent educator and communicator and we all loved her and her style of teaching.

As soon as we moved to Ashdod in July, I found out that I was pregnant. It was a happy surprise; we both were exhilarated about the news. Erekle wanted a baby more than I did and not only him, but his parents were delighted about this unexpected announcement as well. I was the type of girl whose biggest joy was to help her maternal grandmother to take care of her little cousins, feed them, iron their clothes, dress them up, give them a bath, and tuck them into their beds. The devotion I exhibited towards my cousins made me feel that I was ready to have my own child. Erekle and I still had no idea what we were getting ourselves into. We were two kids who were entirely dependent on their parents financially plus already facing so many challenges and obstacles during this overwhelming transition from our homeland to Ashdod, but we decided to bring a new life into the world without any hesitation. In reality, our parents were very supportive and in favor of our decision; hence, we were at ease and not concerned about anything, yet we were clueless about the changes that lay ahead of us.

During the pregnancy, our relationship was becoming intense and more stressful. I was experiencing morning sickness throughout my pregnancy. I was nauseous every morning when we went to school, though at ulpan, during class hours, I used to feel better and always had some snacks with me to nibble on. Unfortunately, Erekle wasn't sympathetic to the fact that I was experiencing all of those pregnancy symptoms. He was annoyed, uneasy, and tensed when I felt unwell. Sometimes he would shout at me while we were walking home from school in public, that's how he tried to suppress and control my symptoms—with his angry voice. Obviously, it didn't work; I was still combatting nausea, but at the same time I was offended, scared, and very hurt. The truth is, on the one hand, he was nervous and worried about my sickness but on the other hand, he didn't know how to handle the condition I was in. So, rather than using the loving part of his personality, he tried to fix my sickness by his aggressive behavior. That's how much he hated me being unwell. From today's perspective, it's crystal clear that he was too young and not ready at all to face all of those tough tests, and so was I. No matter how many times I asked him not to yell at me, my words were worthless. He insulted me anyway, so I attempted not to react to his offensive behavior, particularly outside in the streets. Firstly, I was terribly embarrassed to be yelled at in public and secondly, I was sure that my response would've deteriorated the circumstances, so I chose to stay quiet. Plus, his loud and forceful voice affected me so badly that my entire body would tremble with fear. For that reason, at that time, silence was my best friend. Every time I asked him why he was so angry or shouting at me, he had no specific answer and then he would get angrier and infuriated because I confronted him with my questions. What I recall well is that he hated when I used to say, "I am not feeling well, I might throw up," or if I said, "I am hungry and want to eat out." He would reply to me with a vexed voice, "We can't always eat out; we have to be prudent with our money. We should do our grocery shopping after school and cook when we get home." Neither he nor I knew how to cook and anything that I tried to make at home was so bad that after eating it, I used to vomit almost everything I ate. In spite of that, I obeyed all of his rules because I didn't want to fight or argue with him. Hence, I suffered terribly. Now, I believe that he suffered too, not physically, but emotionally, since the rules that I pointed out above about shopping and cooking at home were not his, but his parents'. And it wasn't about money either because we had a big chunk of cash at home. In addition to that, Erekle's father successfully operated his investments and worked efficiently with other business partners to build an enterprise in Israel. The problem was that every time Erekle spoke with his parents over the phone, they tried to control him by telling him what to do and how to spend our money. He was very secretive and didn't want me to hear what they were telling him on the phone. But once, I was able to hear his father's loud, harsh, and oppressive voice: "Don't spoil her and don't eat out. Let her cook and do housekeeping. You are the man in the house and start taking control." Erekle didn't know that I heard his conversation with his dad, and I never said a word about it. However, I felt very disappointed that they let me down, especially because the promises that his parents made in front of mine, before our marriage, seemed so sincere and real that my parents fully trusted and never doubted them. Moreover, Erekle was tremendously influenced by his parents' opinions and approaches to certain things, and their ill-considered, manipulative, and authoritarian attitude made an enormous impact on him. My father-in-law consistently kept dominating Erekle. He controlled every step Erekle used to make, that's how he displayed his authority and power. Therefore, Erekle imitated his dad and wanted to be in charge of my life as well. However, as Dr. Wayne W. Dyer, an American self-help author and a motivational speaker, said, "A person who has authority never needs to dominate anyone else, ever. A person in a relationship who has to dominate somebody else and has to make the other person submissive shows that they don't have authority because they're getting their power not from within for themselves but on the basis of who they can control and *that never lasts*; the only thing that lasts is having inner power if you will!"[10]

I was too young, inexperienced, and fearful to think deeply and reflect on that. For that reason, I not only allowed Erekle to dominate me, but he let his father do the same to him, due to our fears of being hurt if we didn't obey. As a result, we both had internal conflicts and struggles that heavily affected our relationship.

Furthermore, I didn't want to hurt and dishearten my parents, so I never complained about anything when I spoke with them on the phone. I repeatedly said great things about Erekle and how much I enjoyed my life with him in Ashdod. They were happy that I was doing so well with him and we had everything we needed. Irrespective of that, they still used to send me some money with short notes. I kept almost all of the letters and notes that my parents sent to us in Ashdod. Here is one of the notes they wrote: "Our sweet little girl, we know you and your darling Erekle have everything you need, but we're sending you this money to share with him and spend on anything you both desire. We love you both." Every time Erekle saw the notes with the enclosed money, he would say, "Give that money to me, you don't need it, we can spend it together." Then he would grab the money from my hand without any disagreement or quarrel from my part, as I couldn't stand arguing with him. I preferred being compliant rather than hearing his enraged voice.

∽∞∾

The days were flying by. I was growing bigger and craved for more food each day. Even though I've always been a very picky and fussy eater, the pregnancy totally changed my taste and desire for food. One day, after our last class in ulpan, it was lunch time between 1:00–2:00 p.m. I was very hungry and craved for pizza. The ulpan was located in downtown among many beautiful outdoor cafes and restaurants. Next to our school, there was one of the best outdoor pizza places, where they made the most flavorful, mouth-watering, and fresh pizzas I had ever tasted. Perhaps I loved that place because I was pregnant and developed a selective palate, yet that pizza place was really superb. When we came out of the school building, I could smell the baking crust, the melted cheese, and the scent of oregano, and my appetite increased instantly. That tempting smell of pizza was making me hungry. I told Erekle that the pizza smelled delicious, and it would've been great for lunch. But what I didn't say to him was that I was terribly hungry and didn't have enough energy to do grocery shopping or cooking. You might question me now why didn't I express the way I felt? Why didn't I say the truth? And I agree. I should have, but something was holding me back and that was downright *fear* of being shouted at over pizza (which had happened in the past, so fear was coming from a painful memory). Not only that, but I also feared receiving a negative response from him, which I was anticipating, because he sounded grouchy and miserable. Dr. Joe Dispenza, neuroscientist and an international lecturer, explained, "If you are trying to control and predict when and how it should happen, then you're back in the known. That's because your prediction is more than likely you 'thinking' about some known possibility from your memory of the past and trying to forecast that outcome into the future."[11]

Clearly, I created an undesirable outcome with my fearful thoughts. I was very vulnerable and insecure. As a result, Erekle refused and told me that he couldn't buy pizza all the time, so we needed to go and do our grocery shopping and cook when we got home. Without saying anything, I accepted his decision and continued to walk with him to the grocery store in silence. All the way to the market, I was hungry and longing for that paradise *pizza place*. (Let me be clear here. We didn't eat out all the time and I wasn't an overindulged, spoiled brat who asked him to eat out regularly or to eat in fancy, expensive places and splurge money. The only thing that I really craved for in my pregnancy was *pizza* and it was so affordable for us. The other things we tried to make and cook home whether they turned good or not, that's another story, but at least we made an effort together.) After about fifteen or twenty minutes of walking and dreaming about that heavenly pizza, we reached the market, and as soon as we entered, I lost my consciousness and fainted inside the store. I was hungry and ended up with low blood sugar which made me very dizzy, and I passed out.

Let's rewind and say, for instance, that I was honest and gave Erekle a clear picture of what I truly wanted after school for lunch, which was obviously *pizza*, and I put my entire attention on that and combined it with pleasant emotion rather than having fear and stressing myself about things that didn't happen yet. In that case, I'm sure that the outcome would have been different, much better than what I came across. Actually, for the next few days after this frightening event in the market, Erekle was the sweetest and kindest towards me. He bought me my favorite pizza, did all household chores, and did grocery shopping by himself. At the end of the day, he played guitar for me and sang my favorite songs with his charming voice. His soul was beautiful and loving and that's what kept me hopeful, compassionate, and loving towards him. I attempted not to judge or focus on the negative patterns of his personality.

❧

I've always been very sociable and curious, and the ulpan was the only place where I could get to know other people—immigrants from all over the world. Everyone was so amiable and kind towards us. I loved talking with them, listening to their stories, and learning something from everyone. In Georgia, Erekle had an abundance of friends and he loved hanging out with them; they had lots of fun. In Ashdod, it was quite the opposite; he was constantly with me. Nothing was wrong with that—after all, we were a couple. But I sensed that he was missing his friends' company and I wanted him to be happy and lively like he was in Georgia. Sometimes, it was more apparent, which was completely understandable; don't forget that he was just eighteen years old. In our school, there were a few young guys in the adjacent class. They were also immigrants from Russia and Georgia, and they were very respectful and humble youths. I thought it would have been a great idea if Erekle introduced himself to them. Even though he was introverted and distanced himself from others, at least he would have had somebody to talk with and not feel so gloomy all of the time. For that reason, one day after school, as we were walking down the stairs outside the school building, I noticed that those guys were standing at the corner of the building and interacting with other people. But once they saw us, they paused and looked at Erekle; maybe they thought Erekle and I would stop and introduce ourselves since they used to see us in ulpan every day. As I caught that moment, I took a chance and with an exciting voice, I told Erekle that those fellows were looking at him. Perhaps they wanted to get to know him, and this was a good time to introduce himself to them. Immediately after I finished the sentence, I heard the most raging and wild voice that I had never heard before. He was screaming at me so loud that the entire town could hear him. These were his words: "How could you dare to look at other guys? How do you know that they are interested in knowing me? Don't you fucking dare to look at anyone or anywhere anymore while we walk, otherwise I'll fucking kill you. Do you get me?" I attempted to say something, but he physically pushed me so hard a few times that I almost fell on the ground. In the meantime, he kept screaming, "Shut up and move!" The only thing I wished at that moment was to have a magic wand to make myself disappear forever. I was horribly ashamed and embarrassed in front of others; everyone was looking at us in the street. He wouldn't dare but was ready to physically assault me if I said a word. He bullied and threatened me all the way home. I was ghastly mute and continued walking like a robot. My head was down, staring at the surface of the road; I was extremely afraid and my body was trembling. No one had ever yelled at me or treated me like that in my life. I was devastated and terrified and kept walking towards our apartment building with anxiety. After we got home, he went berserk, throwing things around, slamming doors, punching walls with his fists, spitting all over in the apartment, and yelling incessantly. Then he got all of my shorts and tops from my closet, tore them apart, and threw them through the window. After that, he violently ripped the shirt that I was wearing by pushing and pulling me back and forth and he tossed it into the garbage can while yelling at me. "You will never wear shorts and any of these tops anymore. That's why I'm getting rid of everything and now, because of you, I have a terrible headache and therefore you need to apologize for making me so sick and insane" (periodically, he suffered from migraine headaches). Speaking of my wardrobe, first of all, I was pregnant and was wearing comfortable clothing and secondly, I had never in my teenage years—especially the way I was raised by my parents—wore any inappropriate or vulgar outfits. Lastly, since I had started dating Erekle, I had never flirted with anyone else; that never was my style. Even though I was appalled by his behavior and didn't have a clue what I did wrong, I was utterly ready to apologize for everything to avoid hearing his outrageous voice. I realized that there was no point for me to justify or defend myself or explain anything, because no matter what I said, it would have fueled the fire. He wasn't willing to listen to or hear any statement from me other than an apology. Consequently, I expressed that I was sorry and tried to calm him down. Despite my apology, he was still dissatisfied. He said, "The only way I can forgive you if you go down on your knees and beg me for forgiveness." He spoke such dirty and disgusting words that I had never heard from him previously. He degraded and humiliated me. He wasn't the same person I fell in love with and married. Still, I chose to be forgiven by forcing myself get down on my knees and apologize. Because I was in another country where I didn't speak their language well and I didn't have anyone whom I trusted or could ask for help, I only had my own self to rely on, listen to, and trust. And I didn't have my family there to protect or save me. Therefore, I complied with his request and as soon as I knelt down, I burst into tears and begged for forgiveness as I was on my knees; that was the most mortifying moment for me as a young girl.

The past few years I've been devouring spiritual books, eagerly searching for answers and words of wisdom. I've also been studying and listening to many spiritual teachers, healers, and neuroscientists who have given me the clarity and transparency to every puzzled, confused, and painful circumstance that I have faced in my life and answered almost all of the questions that I have raised along my journey. Being on the path of awakening, practicing living in the present, becoming more conscious, and being connected to my innermost self, has allowed me today to feel deeply compassionate for the pain that Erekle was going through in his teens. He tried to mask his fear and insecurity by expressing his resentment and indignation towards all of his surroundings and all those living in it. Erekle was very young, unconscious, and controlled by his ego. Eckhart Tolle distinctly describes, "When somebody has been taken over by the pain body, it means they're totally asleep, so almost anything you do or say to the pain body will be wrong and it will fuel the fire of the pain body."[12] Now, I'm convinced that in those days, Erekle was taken over by the "pain body" frequently during our relationship, which was often caused by his parents' unconscious, demeaning, and egotistical behavior and attitude towards him. And not only then, but he certainly suffered more as a child by the environment he was raised in. Therefore, it was as much a distressing and terrifying time for him being in another country and starting to build a relationship with me as it was for me. In spite of that, at that time, "the teenage Russo" could never comprehend the reasons why she was treated so abhorrently.

I wasn't present anymore and I wasn't enjoying the days with Erekle like I did prior to our marriage. Although there could've been a remnant of awareness in me, my frightened mind was in charge and as soon as it recognized the danger of being attacked, it shut me off, kept me silent and submissive. According to Gary Zukav:

> "Every experience in your life gives you an opportunity. When a frightened part of your personality is active, you are not conscious. You must be conscious before you can make a choice, which requires an awareness. So, when you are feeling hurt or upset, you can recognize that that's a frightened part of your personality and choose to act from a healthy part of your personality while you're feeling it."[13]

I couldn't reach for the healthiest part of my personality when I was mistreated and abused because, in the first place, I was too young and didn't know *how*; secondly, I wasn't conscious or fully present and my frightened mind was in control most of the time. This meant that not only Erekle was taken over by the "pain body" (ego), and disguised his insecurity and downright fear, but so was I. Thus, *instead of love, I chose fear.*

❧

I was two and a half months pregnant, when my mom surprised me and told me that she was planning to visit us and would stay for around three weeks to help me with my pregnancy. I was more than thrilled to hear that news. My parents had no clue about anything. The only thing they knew was that I was happy in my marriage and Erekle and I were getting along fine. I never desired to disclose any unpleasant information or complain about anything to my parents. My relationship with Erekle was very personal for me; I wanted to deal with that by myself and not forget that it was my decision to be with him and not anybody else's. Additionally, I didn't want my parents to worry about me, so I was very discreet and concealed my nervousness, fearful emotions, and sadness when I talked with them on the phone.

I would never forget how many times Erekle told me the following before my mom arrived in Ashdod: "When the girls get married and once they lose their virginity, it's hard for them to get divorced. In the first place, their parents never want them back, specifically their fathers, because they are ashamed of having a divorced daughter in the house; and secondly, the parents also know that no man would ever desire to marry their daughter, who's not a virgin." There was an innuendo in his statement. What he actually tried to say to me was "Don't complain to your mom when she visits us; she is not going to take you back. You will be an embarrassment to your family." Today, I have a much clearer picture of why he would say that. It was because Erekle had a sister, who was four years older than him. She got married when she was a teenager too, and in a very short period of time, she divorced her husband and went back to her parents. Perhaps Erekle's father was dishonored by having a divorced daughter back home and he might have verbally expressed to his family how abashed he felt. Erekle, as a younger child and sibling, possibly witnessed a wide range of unpleasant, unlovable, and scandalous interactions between his family members, which apparently enormously influenced Erekle's beliefs. Even though at that time I listened to him and understood what he intended to say, I neither challenged him on those words nor strived to prove what I considered was true. I knew that my parents loved me unconditionally and no matter what, they would have been there for me and would have supported me without fail. Although I knew for sure that my parents would have taken me back if I decided to break up with Erekle, his message still affected me profoundly. So, what I believed was that if I ever got divorced, *no man* would desire to be with me or marry me, since I wasn't a virgin anymore. I remember how worthless, unlovable, and cheap I felt. Additionally, I recalled my father's words: "Getting married at this age will not last a long time, maybe around two years, and then you will come back to us and say, 'I can't live with him anymore, it's over.'" I realized that I had only been married about three months and it had already been so intense, hurtful, and physically and emotionally exhausting. In reality, I didn't wish for my father's forecast to come true; besides, in my teenage years, I heard from other adults that the beginning of many marriages was full of challenges, obstacles, and lots of ups and downs. Hence, I was determined to stay optimistic and hopeful in my marriage, as I didn't want to let down my family—primarily my father. In those days, I often asked these questions to myself: What happened to that sweet, kindhearted, and charming Erekle I once knew? How is it possible for someone so loving to become so aggressive, controlling, and hostile? What have I done wrong? On all occasions, I strived to create a peaceful and warm environment in our home. I was very encouraging and supportive towards him and in every aspect of our lives, but nothing was enough for him. One minute Erekle would be absolutely caring and tenderhearted and then unexpectedly, the next minute, his entire personality would change and he would become extremely resentful, wretched, and insulting. Most of the time, Erekle's ill temper and rage erupted so abruptly that I had no clue about why he was getting so furious. As a result, I was becoming more and more fearful and tense in my relationship with him and I was constantly pondering everything before I talked with him. In order to avoid arguments or disagreement, sometimes I even lied about things, because I was scared that the truth might upset him. That's how I guarded myself; I didn't know any other way, and I lived in fear. You can't imagine what was happening in my head. I was creating various plots or scenarios about the same story in my mind and then I would pick the one which was, in my opinion, less troublesome and more acceptable for him. Not only that, but simultaneously I was suppressing all of my torments and hurtful emotions deep inside me so that no one could see the pain I was experiencing; I still tried to remain positive and cheerful.

10

MY MOTHER'S VISIT
ASHDOD, ISRAEL (OCTOBER 1993)

Even though I was very grateful and blessed having my mom with me in Ashdod, I was still worried about her sensing that something was wrong between Erekle and me. However, we both pretended that everything was perfectly fine and that we were taking care of each other well and dealt with other things productively. During my mom's visit, I recognized how much I missed her love, presence, and essence, and of course, her delicious meals. She spoiled us with her care and made all of our favorite dishes. My mom loved Erekle like her own son and for that reason, I didn't want to discourage or sadden her. Nearly every evening, Erekle would play guitar and my mom and he would sing duets together so beautifully that I never wished for those moments to end. Until one day, I was feeling very sick in the morning and decided to stay home. Erekle went to school by himself. After having breakfast, I felt better, and my mom suggested that we go to the park that was close to our apartment and have a little walk. When we came home after a nice stroll, Erekle was already home and he looked grouchy. I thought something happened to him at school and I asked how his day went. He responded to me in an authoritarian manner, and these were his words: "You are my wife and when I come home tired and hungry, I expect you to be here, preparing dinner for me and greeting me and not walking or hanging outside with anyone." Once he finished his expressed request with his controlling voice, I was frozen in time and couldn't open my mouth to say anything, yet my mom replied to him right away with a stern voice, "First, your wife is not your servant or maid to serve you food, you can do it by yourself. Everything was prepared and ready in the kitchen. Second of all, Russo is not your babysitter who sits home and waits for you; you don't need a nanny to feed you. Third, you have no right to raise your voice to her and speak with your wife in an oppressive and domineering way. What kind of attitude is that? Moreover, I am Russo's mother and not *somebody else*. She was with me and it's very disrespectful and rude to talk like that in front of me. And lastly, don't forget that your wife is pregnant and instead of giving her love and care, you are bullying and mistreating her. I'll take her home with me. Since you treated Russo like this in front of me, I can't even imagine how you are treating her without my presence . . . shame on you!" She didn't raise her voice at all even though she was awfully upset. As soon as my mom completed her talk, Erekle got up and, without any comment, promptly left the room. I was sitting at the table speechless; I didn't know what to say. My mom turned towards me and said, "Honey, pack everything and come with me, you can't stay in this condition with him. The way he behaved today, it frightens me for the reason that I don't know how he acts when I'm not here. I am concerned about you and your baby. I know you aren't going to tell me anything, still I'm your mother and I can tell that you are hiding something from me, and it terrifies me. I'm asking you for your own good to come with me back home. Your dad and I will take care of you."

After hearing all of that from my mom, at some point, I was relieved and happy that I could leave everything behind, especially the *fear* that I had in my relationship with Erekle and that I could move back to Georgia. I listened to my mom quietly and what I remember is that I didn't give her any answers then, I just got up and went to my bedroom where Erekle was. The moment I opened the door, I saw Erekle was sitting on the bed and he was crying. I approached him and sat next to him on the edge of the bed. He instantly embraced me and started sobbing like a child and was reiterating these phrases: "Please don't leave me; please don't go with your mom; please don't abandon me . . ." I had never seen Erekle so vulnerable, helpless, and petrified. He was lost in his fears and felt panicky. I didn't leave him—not because I was scared of him at that moment or deeply in love with him in a way that I couldn't live without him, neither of that. Despite my experience with him after marriage, I still cared about him, felt pity, and had compassion for him and at the same time, I didn't desire our breakup to be influenced by my mom or anyone else. I wanted every decision in my personal life to be determined by me; therefore, I chose to stay. (I think what I sensed then was that I still needed to learn more from that relationship, from the path of trials that I took with Erekle, and I knew that the time had not yet come to go back home with my mom.) Although my mom disapproved of my choice, she still respected it and left us peacefully but with much worry and concern. I have huge admiration and appreciation for both of my parents, for not pushing me to do something that I didn't want to do. They respected my decisions, albeit sometimes they didn't favor them.

The next few weeks after my mom's departure, Erekle was more patient, attentive, and tender towards me. At that point in time, the only thing that "little Russo" in me wished was to be loveable and loving. However, from today's viewpoint, I believe that the reason Erekle behaved that way was that he recognized the possibility of losing me; it alarmed and frightened him, not because he was in love with me (although he insisted that he was) but because he needed me. Apparently, my *ego* also discerned the need he had for me and it wanted to please and comfort him so that it would feel adequate and worthy. "It's very easy to confuse love with need, until you recognize that love doesn't hurt, and need does."[14]—Gary Zukav

11

MY FATHER-IN-LAW
ASHDOD, ISRAEL (DECEMBER 1993)

My father-in-law often visited us in Israel since he had to take care of his businesses. He also wanted to see how we were dealing with everything by ourselves. Whenever he spent time with us, I detected that Erekle appeared edgy and tense in his father's presence. What I had observed as a young girl was that my father-in-law was enormously superior to not only Erekle but also to his entire family, because he financially supported everyone and was an affluent businessman. He was excessively conceited. He valued and loved money more than anything else and was terribly greedy, lacking a desire to give. Before my marriage to Erekle, he perfectly concealed those traits in front of my family. Nevertheless, in Ashdod, he didn't hide his domineering and selfish manners. He liked to speak with his son by lowering everyone's dignity and status. He considered himself better and more important than anyone else and so he judged others unfairly. He treated Erekle like a dog, who followed all of his commands, because he *paid* for everything. Unfortunately, he was driven by money and possessions, like an addiction. Even though sometimes Erekle seemed tense and agitated by his father's behavior, particularly when I was present, Erekle never confronted his father. He obeyed and accepted all of his orders and he also imitated his father's style; he absolutely adored him. Undeniably, children are reflections of their parents. As a result, Erekle mirrored his father and regrettably turned into him. He used to say frequently, "All women are after rich men like us; women want nothing but money." These phrases were not his; he was young and copying his father in all aspects and, sadly, believed in those words. Once, I did tell him that I disapproved and objected to his sayings. He ignored and mocked me and repeated the same thing. Deep down, I felt offended and kept reflecting on what he was saying. But at the same time, I was aware that it would have been ineffective to argue with him since he ignored me and didn't care what my beliefs were. He wasn't open or willing to hear anyone else's opinions or perspectives, except for those of his parents. While I'm reminiscing about those days, I feel terribly sad about that young guy who was my husband at that time, who I always believed had a beautiful heart and soul. He had so much love, grace, and benevolence within, yet he buried and compressed them to great depth so that he would never tap into using them.

I was confident that I didn't marry my husband because I was lacking anything, since I grew up with an abundance of love, generosity, prosperity, and joy. I was surrounded by kind and caring people. My parents and grandparents always helped and supported others; my house door was always open to everyone. It still didn't matter to Erekle—he only believed and internalized his parents' principles, rules, and ideology.

While my father-in-law stayed with us, he used to bring his business partners and friends to our place and regularly asked me to prepare meals for his guests. When my mom recently visited, she taught me how to make a few dishes. She also left me some recipes for traditional Georgian cuisine, which I used constantly. I really tried to learn and improve my cooking skills. I had never cooked in Georgia; I didn't need to and had no interest in it either. However, after my marriage, I had a desire to cultivate cooking skills, not because I was passionate for it but I just wanted to fit in, be a good wife, and please Erekle and his father since eating, drinking, and the feast (supra) were, and still are, so essential for Georgians. Moreover, Erekle never liked to help me in the kitchen or with anything while his father was around due to the reason his father considered all housework, cooking, and cleaning a woman's job and he would have made fun of Erekle in front of me if he did any house chores.

One evening, we had visitors from Russia, a couple and two middle-aged men, who were my father-in-law's old friends. The table was set up nicely, though we still had that old oval table with six shaky wooden chairs, and the parts that were broken, Erekle and I had glued them together after we moved into that apartment. But I still hoped that no one would fall and get hurt at dinner time. While everyone was

mingling in the living room, I was still in the kitchen, trying to make Georgian cheese bread (Imeruli Khachapuri,
my favorite). It's a flatbread filled with tender, fresh cheese
that stretches from your mouth as you take a bite. It is one
of Georgia's most popular types of cheese bread. Georgians
usually make this savory pastry with a blend of "Imeruli"
and "Sulguni" cheese, but a mixture of feta and low-moisture
mozzarella can get you very close to the traditional version.
So, I was doing my best to make it tasty and flavorful, to de-
light our guests. In fact, if you want to be good at anything in
your life, you need to practice it and practice it a lot, without
question. I was a complete novice, still learning and growing in each field every day. Shortly after the guests' arrival,
Erekle came into the kitchen to grab some drinks and while
getting the drinks, he snatched a small piece of cheese bread
from the serving dish and devoured it. Then he looked at me
and said, "What a shit you made," and he walked out at once.
I was stunned and unable to react. I didn't know what to do;
I definitely didn't want to be embarrassed in front of everyone. Swiftly, I took a tiny piece of cheese bread and tasted it
as I was pacing back and forth in the kitchen; surprisingly it
wasn't that bad. It was OK and eatable, surely not like my
mother or my grandmothers used to make, yet it was alright.
Among all of those male guests, there was a young Russian
lady, in her early forties, named Tatiana. She was an elegant,
strong, intelligent, very generous, financially independent,
and well-accomplished woman. She and her husband were
very old friends of my father-in-law. I met Tatiana a few times
prior to this visit and I had huge respect for her. Each time

we met, her presence brought me so much serenity, faith, and strength. Tatiana was the type of woman who represented the archetype of a kind and compassionate guardian. She was so trustworthy and I wished to be like her—strong, free, and independent. Apparently, she witnessed the whole scene with my husband and came into the kitchen and offered me her help. Although she only spoke Russian, she understood what went on with Erekle and she sensed my vibe. I was sad, weary, and dispirited but I still gave her a smile and thanked her for her kind gesture. She was an exceptionally supportive and loving woman. Immediately after talking with me, she called my father-in-law into the kitchen and told him firmly, with an upset voice, that it was unfair and inconsiderate to have a pregnant teenager standing and cooking for six people all by herself in the kitchen. She said that instead of cooking for them, I should be resting or taking a nice walk with my husband at the beach or studying and doing my homework for school. She really sounded disappointed about the circumstances. Anyway, my father-in-law's response was brief and precise, "When a *woman* gets married, she has to know how to cook and how to take care of her family." (In those days, men considered that most of the chores at home should be done by women.) That comment produced more irritation and resentment within Tatiana. She replied stiffly in Russian, "You call Russo a *woman* who is supposed to know how to cook? Wow!" After saying that, she ended that conversation there. She didn't want to turn the evening into a conflict zone but what she really wished for me was the same thing she wished for her own daughter, who was exactly my age. Later that evening, she spoke with me privately. First, she told me fleetingly about her daughter, how much she enjoyed college in London, and how happy she was over there. Then she showed me some of her photos with her college friends. She said how vital it was for every girl to acquire an education and pursue their dreams. She continued that girls' education was essential and good, educated women could be healthier, potent, self-sufficient, and secure and that they most certainly were able to educate their own children. She didn't want to focus on my relationship with Erekle; albeit, at times, she noticed his unpleasant behavior, yet she knew that it wasn't her job to interfere or judge my marriage or to influence me with her beliefs. She was there for only one reason—to empower and encourage me as a young girl so I could become the woman I deserved to be. Now, I firmly believe that this beautiful universe always sends us helpers and guides along our journey, especially when we need them the most and it's up to us to recognize them. On that day, I didn't recognize the power of her message; however, her words were engraved in my mind forever. Since then, I started visualizing acquiring an education and I immensely wished to study in London, one of the most beautiful cities in the world. Tatiana showed up as a magical helper, who was there only for a short period of time, but her influence on my life made a significant impact that lasted throughout my journey.

Two days later, I felt very depressed, fatigued, and low-spirited when I woke up. Erekle was already in school, my father-in-law was gone, as he had some business meetings, and I was by myself in the apartment. I didn't want to get up. I just longed to stay all alone in bed and hated the idea that I needed to cook again for everyone. At some point, I even wished I wasn't pregnant anymore and hoped to have a miscarriage. I was overwhelmed, mentally and physically exhausted, and overly disheartened. In my mind, I kept ruminating on the same thing—how to make an excuse for not cooking that day. My mother used to tell me *all the time*, "'No' is a very important word and sometimes, you need to use it. If you can't do something or even if you don't want to do something, simply say, 'No, I'm sorry, but I can't do it.' If you keep agreeing and saying 'yes' to everything, people will take advantage of you and eventually you will be hurt, because you were not honest with yourself." Irrespective of my mom's advice, I was still unable to use that word because, since my childhood, it was my disposition and nature to help, serve, and care for others. By saying "No, I can't," I didn't wish to hurt, upset, or disappoint anyone. As a consequence, I came up with an agenda to make myself sick, so I could scare Erekle and his father when they came home and they would not ask me to do anything. However, I was aware of a strong medication called *diazepam* that Erekle used to take for his awful migraine headaches and it helped him a lot. This medication is a benzodiazepine, a tranquilizing muscle relaxant, used mostly to relieve anxiety. Hence, I snatched the small container from the bathroom cabinet, took out a handful of pills and instantly shoveled them into my mouth. I was so desperate and though I had never ever had an intention to kill myself, I just wanted to look sick. In those days,

I was *clueless* and had no knowledge about how an overdose of diazepam (or any medication) could have been fatal. After shoving all of those pills into my mouth, I wasn't able to swallow them all together and started choking on them. Luckily, I began throwing up and puked everything out at once. I was a mess, standing in the bathroom and washing myself in the sink, and at the same time, I felt relieved that I was alive and survived that insane plan. Despite this failed attempt, I continued pursuing my second goal, which was to induce a miscarriage. The only thing that I was aware of was that during pregnancy, the body was in a fragile state and rigorous exercises could cause natural miscarriage. Thus, the first thought that came into my mind was to stand on a chair and jump. I did jump a few times and then stopped, as I started feeling a little weak and lightheaded. But I was lucky again, since that wobbly chair didn't collapse on me. In spite of those dangerous and crazy attempts on that day, fortunately, I remained alive and healthy, and surprisingly, neither of the plans worked. I didn't look sick when Erekle and my father-in-law came home, so *I still cooked and served them.* "The law of attraction is this: You don't attract what you want. You attract what you are."—Dr. Wayne W. Dyer

12

MY BABY BOY ARRIVED
ASHDOD, ISRAEL (APRIL 1994)

I was really blessed that my son was born one hundred percent healthy. He was my miracle baby, who brought me extraordinary strength and courage. We officially named him Teymuraz, after my father-in-law (in Georgian tradition, the first son is usually named after his paternal grandfather). However, Erekle and I were reluctant to call him Teymuraz. We felt that the name was too formal and unsuitable for him. After searching for nicknames, Erekle finally settled on "Chiko" and I loved it! (In Spanish, *chico* means a small boy or child; we just changed the letter C to K to make it more distinctive.) Chiko was a sweet little boy and the name was spot on.

The postpartum period was extreme for me. After coming home from the hospital with a newborn baby, I wasn't only sore and weary but stressed about having my mom and my mother-in-law, Manana, together in the apartment.

While my mom, who's the most loving and nurturing person in the world, strived to help me with utterly everything, Manana kept complaining and finding fault in everything my mom did. Her tactless remarks and troublesome manner overwhelmed my mom and made her step back during her stay. For example, Manana would say that my mom didn't know how to hold a baby properly or how to bathe a newborn and put him to sleep. Sometimes, when my mom was holding Chiko, Manana would snatch the baby from her hands and walk vigorously around the room, criticizing my mother. This was her attempt to influence Erekle that she was a more caring grandmother, who knew how to take care of the baby better than my mom. For Manana, everything was a competition; she was jealous that my mother was there for Chiko and me. Despite all of that, my mom never reacted to Manana's impertinent and insensitive behavior. She essentially ignored it since she has always been against conflict and under any circumstance, she would rather walk away quietly than having an argument with anyone. In addition to that, she didn't want to aggravate my relationship with my husband and Manana. So, because of that, she chose to leave Israel peacefully. One morning, she came into my room when no one else was home and told me, "My girl, you know how much I love you, but in order to keep a healthy balance and peace in this house, I should go. I apologize that I'm not able to help you more with your baby, but this is the best way to deal with this toxic situation. You are young, brave, and smart, and you need to make your own decisions for yourself and for your baby. If I stay around Manana any longer, I will get sick. Her presence, judgments, and actions affect me terribly. No matter what, I want you to remember that your father and I are always here for you and Chiko." I was glad that my mom made that decision, although I immensely needed her help at that time. Yet, I loved her more and her health and well-being were a priority for me. I didn't want her around Manana either. Even though on the inside, I was overly emotional, I stayed brave and tearless and told her not to worry and that Chiko and I would be perfectly fine.

When my mom left, all of my fears of not knowing what to do, or not being able to take care of my son without her help, instantly disappeared. Once I held my baby in my arms and looked at his wide brown eyes, I felt my inner strength and I had faith that I would become as caring and a loving mother as my mom was.

❦

It was almost the end of August 1994, four months after Chiko was born, when I found out that my mother- and sister-in-law planned to visit us in Ashdod. The news didn't really excite me but since Erekle loved his mom and sister and was thrilled about their visit, I acted that I was happy too. My sister-in-law hadn't yet had a chance to visit us in Ashdod and this was a great opportunity for her. Her name was Eka and, at that time, she was twenty-three years old and a graduate student. She was very attractive and witty. When they arrived, I welcomed them with warmth and kindness. They enjoyed staying with us and loved the city of Ashdod.

However, a couple of weeks later, my mother-in-law made a big announcement for a long-term stay. That was so unexpected and such shocking news for me because I knew that she was still working as an optometrist in Georgia. Despite that, I stayed silent and pretended that I was pleased. Erekle's parents covered all of the expenses, including the apartment, so I had no right to say anything since Erekle, Chiko, and I were dependent on them. I didn't mind my sister-in-law's company that much. She was young, free, and easy to be around; besides, she started taking Hebrew language classes at the ulpan, which kept her busy and active. But living with my mother-in-law was turning into a nightmare.

13

LIVING WITH MY MOTHER-IN-LAW
ASHDOD, ISRAEL (1994)

I distinctly remember how much I wanted to breastfeed Chiko, but my milk supply wasn't even close to adequate for a newborn, so I was encouraged by my doctor to supplement with formula. And shortly after, because of the stress and exhaustion, my milk fully dried out. From then on, I needed to get up a few times during the night to prepare Chiko's food. One night, I was so drowsy from sleepless nights and when I got up from my bed, I walked to the kitchen with my eyes closed. Suddenly, I crashed into the wall. I hit my forehead so hard that I lost balance and almost fainted on the floor. I crouched down for a few minutes, then got up slowly, and proceeded to my job in the kitchen. I prepared a bottle as fast as I could, as Chiko kept crying; he was hungry and was waiting for me. The next morning, I had a huge red bump on my forehead. Everyone laughed at me and told me how stupid I was that I couldn't walk properly in the house.

Erekle rarely helped me during the nights with Chiko. Once he had helped, when I was really sick during the first month after Chiko's birth and I had a very high fever. On other occasions, his mother used to say that he needed to sleep well at night, as he got up early, went to school, and then he needed to study and complete his homework. At some point, she even told him to move to her bedroom so he could get a good night's rest; she said my sister-in-law could stay with me in my bedroom. Almost every night, shortly after we used to go to bed, Manana would aggressively open our bedroom door without knocking, come into the room, and give Erekle a good-night kiss. Sometimes she asked him very trivial questions that she could have asked during the day. As a young girl, I had the feeling that she was very jealous that Erekle was sleeping with me. She kept bringing up the same topic with Erekle, about switching the bedrooms with his sister, because she wanted him to sleep well at night. Ultimately, she got her way and made him move to her bedroom while Eka moved to mine. The possessiveness that Manana exercised on his son was transparent. Erekle generally listened to whatever she said; he adored her and followed all of her instructions. I didn't interfere, as I sensed how much power she had over her children, so I chose to remain silent. Her control over him was absolute. She expected Erekle to check in with her before he made any decisions, and she violated his privacy by looking at his personal things in his room. He didn't object to any of this but followed her direction blindly.

While Erekle was in ulpan in the mornings, I liked to leave a sweet little note secretly on his desk, where he used to study every day. I knew that he would appreciate it when he came home. He loved getting those small, fun, and witty notes from me; surprisingly, at the beginning when my mother- and sister-in-law moved to Ashdod, Erekle was more loving and tender towards me. One morning, when Erekle and Eka were at school, I was going to put a small card on Erekle's desk and when I entered the room, Manana was sitting at the desk searching for something. She didn't expect me and felt a little awkward when I showed up. So, instantaneously, I turned around and left the room. But she called me back and told me that she wrote a little note for Erekle and wanted to hide it somewhere on his desk to surprise him. I responded to her with a fake smile that it was nice of her to do that and promptly walked out of the room. My heart was racing; I immediately tore up my little card that I was discreetly holding in my hand, then quickly readied Chiko's stroller, grabbed my baby, and went to the park for a walk. I needed to breathe.

❧

My in-laws were gourmands—they loved to cook and eat but they hated to clean. They could stay in a filthy apartment for a long time without a problem. On top of that, Manana and Erekle were very heavy smokers. I neither smoked nor could stand the dirt, dust, or scent of cigarettes in the apartment. Since I wasn't cooking and Manana used to cook for all of us, I decided to please her and took the responsibility for cleaning the entire house. That's how I conveyed my appreciation to her. I endeavored to eliminate an unpleasant musty odor in our home by ceaseless deep-cleaning all the time. I wanted to make sure that my baby breathed fresh air and lived in a neat place. Once everyone noticed that I was always eager to organize, wash, and clean everything (not only for my baby but for everyone), they became indolent. My sister-in-law would throw banana skins underneath her bed with other garbage and keep them there forever. My in-laws never cleaned their bathrooms or bedrooms, or anything, and they could stay in bed until 1:00 or 2:00 p.m. Erekle got worse and never helped me around his family either. The disgusting dirt and disorder didn't really bother them, but it bothered me, badly. So, instead of waiting for them to do anything, I took care of everyone's filth and mess. As a result, my in-laws nicknamed me "sponge." I didn't have any reaction to that because as long as I took care of everyone's clutter, they were nice to me. I carried on with pleasing them. However, I was getting overly exhausted from everything—not sleeping at night, taking care of Chiko during the day, cleaning, and sometimes doing grocery shopping. Nevertheless, what became unbearable for me was that Manana was hypercritical. She found faults in everything and incessantly kept correcting me about every little thing; for instance, the way I was dressing up or fixing my hair or doing my makeup or making my bed or even about which pj's I should or shouldn't wear! She hated the ones that my mom bought me, yet I loved and wore them often. She used to say that there was too much red in them. And she would disfavor the way I was dressing up Chiko or even holding the spoon to feed him. In every little detail, she could point out errors and she sought out faults in everyone. She would correct me about how to use and hold the mop; She would also point out faults in the way I folded clothes or bedsheets and placed them in the drawers; and she endlessly checked my closet, which was immaculately organized. Perhaps she was seeking some errors in there too. Imagine every single day someone watching and correcting you a thousand times about every little thing, telling you how to wash, clean, dress, eat, or even breathe; how would you feel? How did I feel? Horrible, overly stressed, and worn out. One day while Erekle and his mother were sitting at the dining table and smoking and I was making vegetable soup in the kitchen for Chiko, I inadvertently left a metal spoon with veggies and some water in the blender when I turned it on. The blender literally exploded, and the kitchen walls, floor, my face, and clothes were splattered and fully covered with soup. I wasn't frightened or hurt by it but what really shattered me was the wild and uncontrolled yelling at me by Manana and Erekle. Because their verbal abuse caused me so much distress instead of unplugging the blender quickly, I anxiously pushed the "on" button again. I was *so lost*! I didn't know what I was doing and I thought they were going to kill me.

It's easy to blame and hate my mother-in-law for many reasons and it's even easier to fall into troubles, fears, and self-pity, which are all signs of weakness, insecurities, and primarily unconsciousness. In one of his best-known works, *As a Man Thinketh,* James Allen, a British philosophical writer, narrated:

> "A man's weakness and strength, purity and impurity, are his own, and not another man's; they are brought about by himself, and not by another; and they can only be altered by himself, never by another. His condition is also his own, and not another man's. His suffering and his happiness are evolved from within."[15]

Because I was constantly controlled by my fearful thoughts, I was powerless to speak up and say the truth— how I felt or how I wanted to do certain things or manage my own life. For instance, when Manana dominated me and ran my daily schedule, when she incessantly corrected me on every little detail, when my in-laws called me names or told me what to wear, how to fix my hair, or do my makeup, I complied with them. I didn't want to hurt their feelings and I never wished them harm. I wanted to give my love and to be loved by them. But what I was unaware of then was that by staying submissive, being untruthful to myself, and by not having enough courage to speak up and say the word "no," I was hurting and betraying my own self. Consequently, *the condition, and suffering that I was in, was brought on by me and not by them. My suffering and unhappiness were evolved from within.*

My mom, who was my guardian, teacher, and best friend, was there for me and offered her help twice in Israel, yet I didn't accept it. She respected my decision and therefore she walked away. As James Allen further described:

> "A strong man cannot help a weaker unless that weaker is willing to be helped, and even then the weak man must become strong of himself. He must, by his own efforts, develop the strength which he admires in another. None but himself can alter his condition."

So, my mom allowed me to learn on my own and didn't interfere in my relationship, regardless of my age. Although my mother physically wasn't in Ashdod with me during the most frightful time in my life, I still felt her loving energy and was aware that she was watching over me. The difference between my mom and me though was that she could say *no*, if she wanted to without hesitation. She could speak up and say what she desired. She respected herself and knew her own values and didn't hide her truth within herself; whatever she *asked, she always received*, because fear didn't rule her. "Ask, and it shall be given you."[16] Having my mother as a parent, I should have been brimming with self-love, self-respect, and confidence; unfortunately, I wasn't. I had to learn on my own—I had to become strong by myself. And by *my own efforts I needed to develop the strength that I admired in my mom and others.*

As days and months went on, my life in Ashdod was turning more daunting. I needed to ask permission from my mother-in-law every time I wanted to do something. If I was interested in taking my son to the park or simply going out for a walk with my sister-in-law, I had to get Manana's approval. Otherwise, she would complain to Erekle that I was disrespectful to her. The worst part was that I couldn't call my family freely. I needed to get Erekle's *and* Manana's consent to call my parents from the house phone. And while I was talking with them, Erekle and my in-laws would watch me and listen to every word I said. When I spoke with my mom and dad, I was under pressure so I couldn't say much. The only thing I could say was that I was fine and we were all doing very well. I was micromanaged and inspected for every step I took while I was living in Ashdod. Sometimes, I was allowed to do grocery shopping by myself; Erekle or Manana would give me cash but after shopping, they would check my receipt and count the change. They always made sure that I had no leftover money. The money that my parents left for my son and me after Chiko's birth was taken away from me as well. Erekle and his family were obsessed about possessions and money. Numerous times I witnessed how compulsively they counted a big chunk of cash then bought plenty of gold, expensive jewelry, clothes, and various gadgets. Manana was addicted to gold bracelets and she endlessly purchased them along with other "things" during her stay in Ashdod. I lived in the beautiful country of Israel for almost two years with my husband, Chiko, and my in-laws and, it's a shame to say but I never visited any other place, not a single museum, and not even one of the world's oldest and holiest cities—Jerusalem. Fortunately, two years prior to my move to Ashdod, my mom, my brother, and I had traveled to Israel and we had a marvelous time exploring different cities and many of the historic sites within the country, so I do have some good memories of Israel.

Because of their greed and selfishness, my in-laws and Erekle stored away money, gold, and diamonds like squirrels burying nuts for the winter. Erekle once threatened me and said, "I know exactly how much money I have and if I ever see you taking a penny from my drawer, you know what will happen to you." I assumed he would kill me and of course, not once did I touch or ask for money. I didn't want anything from them. Whatever my parents had brought for Chiko and me was enough for both of us. I've never been materialistic or money-oriented and, particularly that time, I just wanted love, peace, freedom, laughter, and my *mom and dad*. Chiko was my only light in the darkness around me. He was the only one who uplifted my spirit when I felt sad, and he put a smile on my face when I wanted to cry. He was my little angel, whose existence ultimately encouraged me enough to start praying for guidance and clarity.

In the evenings, after putting Chiko to sleep, Manana used to sit close to her children and speak very softly to them, almost whispering. Each time I entered the living room, she would look at me as if I was a stranger in the house and Eka and Erekle did the same. Then they would pause and stay silent until I went back to my bedroom. But there were also times when they wanted me to hear what they were saying. They would raise their voices while I was in the kitchen, preparing Chiko's food, and say things like I was a silly and unintelligent girl who knew nothing; to them, I was nobody. They all used offensive language and swore a lot. Their avoidance of me and distancing from me made it unquestionable that I wasn't part of that family. I was just there to clean, serve, and obey all of their rules. At last, I recognized that Erekle was never going to be there for Chiko or me; he didn't care about us. He had no idea what he really wanted in his life; he was lost and disoriented by his mother's fanatic love and her unhealthy relationship with him.

I would go to my bedroom each evening, put Chiko to sleep, and then would drop to my knees, bend my head down on the floor, start crying and praying quietly, so nobody could hear me. One night, while on my knees, I prayed and asked God these questions: "Is this how my life is going to stay? Am I going to live like this from seventeen to forever? Is this what I chose for myself?" I recall it so clearly that when I asked those questions, I instantly heard my own self speaking bravely from within. "No, I don't want to live like this anymore. I want to go back and live with my parents and raise my baby in a loving, generous, compassionate, and caring environment. I want to go to college, get a decent education, and become an independent and strong woman. And above all, I want to have enough money to take care of myself and my son so that I would never be in a position, in a relationship or in a marriage, where I feel trapped or controlled."

I would like to point out here again that once you ask, you will receive answers. Even though, at that time, I didn't understand the power of asking or receiving or being present or connected to my true essence, what I did perceive was that I listened to and allowed myself to receive the answers. I was given clarity after my prayers. I also acknowledged that Erekle and his family would have been a bad influence over Chiko, and unequivocally, I didn't want to raise my son around them.

Hence, the first thing I decided to do was to call my mom and inform her about my decision. I knew that calling my mom from the house phone and telling her my plans was impossible; however, I came up with another plan, which was challenging too. First, I needed to find a payphone outside somewhere, in a safe place where my in-laws could not see me. This wasn't that difficult or unmanageable, but what was really problematic was to obtain some cash for change. If I asked Erekle or Manana for some money, they would have been suspicious as to why I needed it and, in all likelihood, they would have followed me when I took Chiko out for a walk. This was troublesome and I don't know what they would have done to me if I wasn't obedient and sweet to them. For me, going to the park every morning and breathing without fear was the only freedom that I had, and I certainly didn't want to be deprived of that. So, I cautiously started collecting change in the apartment. My sister-in-law always had a lot of cash and change and sometimes she would be forgetful and leave coins in random places or drop them in the apartment. So, little by little, I collected some of the change, but not all of it so no suspicion was raised. Erekle did the same thing; on occasion, he would leave change in his pants pockets or other places that he forgot about. I would take only a few coins so it wasn't too noticeable. Finally, I accumulated more than enough change to contact my parents. The first phone call that I made from the outside payphone was extremely emotional for me as well as for my mom. Once I heard her voice, I burst out crying. I was standing in the phone booth, clasping my baby close to my heart, and looking intensely around, making sure that I would not be caught by anyone. Chiko was staring at me silently with his big brown eyes, as if he felt everything that I felt in that moment. I told my mom that I couldn't stand *that family*, I couldn't breathe or live with *them* any longer. I wanted to go back home to my parents' house, and told her *this marriage* was over. My mom was expecting this outburst and admission from me at some point in time, yet she waited for me to approach her for help. She calmed me down in her loving and nurturing way and promised me that she and my dad would do everything to take Chiko and me back home together. In the meantime, she asked me to stay patient, calm, and strong. My mom's intention was to take care of everything in a wise, peaceful, and civil manner without drama or war between our two families. Additionally, at that point in time, my parents were in the process of moving to Turkey, where my father launched a small business, and they were going to begin a new life in a modern and historic city—Istanbul.

After that emotional conversation with my mom, a few days later, I heard a phone call discussion between my in-laws. They talked about the visitor's visa that my mom requested from my father-in-law for her to come to Israel. When Manana asked if there was any reason why my mom decided to visit us so unexpectedly, he told her that my mother just missed Chiko and me terribly. My mom knew that if she expressed dissatisfaction or annoyance about anything, I would've gotten into trouble. In order to protect me, she kept everything simple and uncomplicated. A week later, when I called her again, my mom told me that my father-in-law promised to get her a visa very soon, which made me very hopeful.

Time was flying by and life in Ashdod was turning more and more unbearable. Manana's toxic manner continued to intimidate me but I stayed optimistic and put all of my focus on how to reunite with my parents in Turkey. At the same time, I carried on with my daily duties with a nice but benign demeanor. Almost a month passed by and my mom still didn't have a visa to come to Ashdod. By that time, I was certain that Erekle and my in-laws didn't want her to come to see Chiko and me. I was devastated and didn't know what to do. I asked God for help and prayed for a miracle every night, and finally it happened.

It was the second week of December 1994. One afternoon, Erekle returned home early from school and he looked emotionally drained. We found out that he got involved in a major fight with some guys at school and they threatened him really badly. He didn't tell us the details about the whole thing but I was convinced that it was very, very serious because he told us that we needed to leave Ashdod as soon as possible and move to Turkey, where my parents were. Erekle told me that we could stay temporarily with my parents and then rent a place on our own. He looked exceedingly panicked and nervous, which obviously alarmed Manana. The news stunned me; I couldn't believe that this was really happening and I genuinely thought that I was dreaming this whole thing. I stood there still listening to Erekle and slowly digesting this unbelievable news. Even though I was scared too, and truly didn't want Erekle to get harmed, I wanted to scream, dance, and jump for joy, knowing that very soon I could rejoin my parents. Regardless of that, I stayed calm and conveyed my empathy for the circumstance that Erekle was going through. Needless to say, I didn't wish any of his family to see or feel that I was exhilarated about moving to Turkey. They could have changed their mind, so I was very careful how I acted.

The next day, my mother-in-law called her husband in Georgia and informed him about the situation with Erekle and that we needed to leave Ashdod as soon as possible. My father-in-law supported our decision and told us to move to Turkey immediately. I'm sure you can imagine now how my parents celebrated this unbelievable and surprising news. They couldn't wait to see Chiko and me.

We didn't have that much time yet we had so much to do in the apartment. We needed to arrange, pack, and ship many things thus we needed tons of boxes. Erekle was very concerned and frightened to go out anywhere. Eka was lazy; she didn't want to help me to go get boxes or take care of anything outside, but she was willing to pack, which was helpful but impossible without boxes. I can't blame Manana since she didn't speak Hebrew and she had no idea where to go or what to do. She was totally dependent on Erekle and her husband so clearly, nothing was moving forward. I realized that if I followed their pace, we would be stuck in Ashdod for quite a while. So, I took all of the responsibility of returning items, recycling what I could, collecting boxes, etc., whatever needed to be done outside of the apartment, I took care of it. We needed a variety of different sized boxes and wrapping paper. I got a few from some grocery markets but I didn't know where else to go, whom to ask, or how to get them. But I noticed that a big supermarket located close to my apartment building had outdoor dumpsters and trash cans at the rear of the building. Next to them, I saw big cardboard boxes that seemed in good shape to still be useable. I got so excited even though the whole building, including the backside, was secured by tall metal fences so no one could enter the supermarket's property. It was getting late; I rushed home and told Manana that I found some cardboard boxes and that I needed her to come with me. Without delay or questions, she immediately got up and followed me. I didn't notice it then, but now I know that was the first time that she recognized my confidence and toughness. She was consumed by fear about her son and this move, but my ability to take control of what needed to be done outside actually made her nicer and more supportive of me. I think, she finally felt that I was capable of doing other things as well. When we got to the back of the market, I told her that I was going to jump over the fence and grab the huge cardboard boxes, because the next morning, a garbage truck would pick up and recycle them, and they would be gone. Also, I told her if she saw anyone walking towards us, she should alert me right away. She agreed and totally backed me up with my little plan. She stood there and watched me climbing up on that tall metal fence. I loved climbing all kinds of trees in my childhood and sitting on various branches for hours, so I utilized my acquired skills during this little caper. Even though those fences were very hard to climb on, I still made it; I scaled the fence and jumped over it, quickly seized those large cardboard boxes, then threw them over the fence one by one.

Each of us has a task in this life and sometimes we find it impossible to complete, but once we are provoked, we discover our unlimited inner strength to accomplish anything.

Jean Houston's encouraging words teach us "No matter what adventures (good or ill) we encounter on our journeys, all have been divinely orchestrated by us in order to assist us in our growth as human beings on Earth and our expansion as souls. We learn through experience, not theory alone."[17]

As I look back and think about my ex-mother-in-law now, I have a clearer insight about her behavior and persona. She was a very unhappy married woman. Her husband never showed her love, affection, care, or respect. I witnessed many times how reckless and inconsiderate my father-in-law was to his wife. He constantly cheated on her and had affairs with many other women. He had addiction problems as well.

Manana was aware of all of this and even discussed her personal issues with her children. Every time she spoke about her husband, I could sense that she still loved him regardless of everything he put her through. She praised how handsome, charming, and irresistible he was. He surely was a good-looking man and Manana was a very attractive woman, she was educated and a well-trained doctor, who came from a well-respected family too. Unfortunately, she was addicted to money and possessions, as was my father-in-law, so I believe that was one of the core reasons why they stayed together. They both hoarded money and consistently wanted more; what they had was never enough. Therefore, neither of them was content and they were miserable together. However, Manana was so wounded and damaged that her unhealthy relationship with her husband resulted in hurting her children's relationships. She was in so much pain that she didn't want to see happiness in anyone's life around her. In these years, I was too young to be aware of her suffering and the cause of her envious and spiteful manners, but now I absolutely do. Presently, I am empathetic towards her and I wish she valued, respected, and loved herself more than anything else so that she could have had a loving, compassionate, healthy, and happy relationship with her children. Gary Zukav describes:

> "Every addiction exists for one reason and one reason only and that is to cover pain, to mask a terrible, excruciating, inexplicable, undefinable, and an unbearable pain. Every addictive

behavior serves the purpose of masking that pain at least temporarily. The only way to heal an addiction, and that means to move beyond its control, is to be able to find the pain that addiction is attempting to mask."[18]

I believe both of my in-laws were covering their tormenting and unfathomable pain through their dependency and addiction towards money and they were unable to find and heal the pain that their addiction attempted to mask. They stayed together for their entire life, accumulating and hoarding more money and possessions. After my separation with Erekle in 1995, I never saw my father-in-law again. Unfortunately, he suffered terribly from cancer for several years and in 2017, he lost his battle and passed away. In 2017, I still remembered the hurt and up to that time, I blamed him for many things. Despite that, when I found out about his death, I felt sorry and truly wanted to forgive him. Although I expressed forgiveness verbally with myself, something was missing; I wasn't fully honest with myself, since I was still attached to my past memories. In his book *The Power of Now: A Guide to Spiritual Enlightenment*, author Eckhart Tolle clearly explains:

"You cannot truly forgive yourself or others as long as you derive your sense of self from the past. Only through accessing the power of the Now, which is your own power, can there be true forgiveness. This renders the past

powerless, and you realize deeply that nothing you ever did or that was ever done to you
could touch even in the slightest the radiant
essence of who you are. The whole concept
of forgiveness then becomes unnecessary."[19]

Before I was able to access the power of the Now, I
had to proceed on the road of challenges that lay ahead.

14

REUNITING WITH MY PARENTS
ISTANBUL, TURKEY (JANUARY 1995)

Reuniting with my parents in Turkey made me feel like I was reborn. In January 1995, starting a new life in the glamorous city of Istanbul, one of the world's largest cities by population and the most populous city in Turkey, with my son, mom, and dad was a dream come true.

Istanbul is a transcontinental city in Eurasia, straddling the Bosporus strait (which divides Europe and Asia) between the Black Sea and the Sea of Marmara. About the third of the city's population lives in suburbs on the Asian side of the Bosporus, and on the European side lies the city's historical and commercial center.[20]

My parents lived in a cozy and delightful apartment in the suburbs on the Asian side close to the Sea of Marmara. The day when we arrived at my parents' place (although Erekle and my in-laws were there with me), I sensed that I was completely relieved from the heaviest load I carried for almost a year and a half and I was the happiest girl on earth. When my parents first saw me, they couldn't recognize me. I looked so sleep-deprived and fatigued that I was barely holding my nine-month-old baby in my arms. My dad was hardly holding his rage; he seemed almost ready to explode and throw Erekle and my in-laws out of the apartment, but he tried to control his temper. My parents still respectfully welcomed them all and didn't want to act on how they felt—enraged and upset. They stayed patient, calm, and kind and at the same time, they hoped that my in-laws would go back to Georgia soon so Erekle and I could determine how to move on with our lives. Alternatively, my in-laws' intention was to stay in Istanbul with us and explore the city. They had no reason or plan to leave and they loved my parents' tidy place. Everything was taken care of; my mom cooked for everyone and helped me with Chiko during the day and night as well. Furthermore, my in-laws spent most of the days in their bedroom sleeping, reading, and eating, but some fragments of a day they would go out. They did some shopping and familiarized themselves with the new city. However, I was convinced that they would never leave us alone in peace and they would never move back to Georgia or anywhere else. My parents weren't happy about that but they also didn't want to reveal their dissatisfaction and frustration so they remained tranquil and tolerant, as did I. I let go of resistance and focused on all of the blessings that I was receiving from my parents. What mattered to me the most was that Chiko and I were protected and safe with my parents.

Now, I want to share with you the secret that I've never disclosed to anyone besides my mom and a couple of very dear friends. My grandmother once told me an old myth about the broom that is passed along in certain cultures all over the world. She spoke about a few beliefs concerning the broom and one of them was if I ever wanted to prevent an undesirable guest from returning, I had to sweep out the hallway after they left the house. I recalled my grandmother's words and started pursuing my goal. Every time my in-laws left the apartment, I vigorously swept the hallway and laughed at myself while doing it. I thought I was hilarious by following the myth. In my childhood, I always believed in magic and miracles, and above all, the smallest things used to inspire me fully. I believed that there were angels, fairies, and invisible helpers around me, assisting and supporting me all the time. Today, I absolutely believe that there are invisible helpers, angels, fairies, whatever you label them, around every living being in this world, who gently guide and help each and every one of us to learn and grow on the roads of ordeals in our lives. Indeed, there are circumstances and situations that get darker and become perilous on our paths, but it is the darkness that awakens and evolves us and that's where we discover our strengths. In the midst of writing this book, I wrote the following poem:

The World within Us
Some stars are brighter than others,
Some are too far to see.
It's not what we can perceive with

Our own eyes—
The unseen prompts us to imagine and dream.
The world that has an infinite source of wisdom,
Intelligence, power, wealth, and more—
That world lies only within us;
We can find it when we get
In touch with our souls.
There is no person in this world that finds
This life unchallenging or pain-free.
There is no journey and no path that always shines—
It is the darkness that evolves us
And makes us strong and real.

It was early morning, around the third week of January 1995; my father was at work when we received an unanticipated phone call from Georgia. One of my in-laws' relatives called and informed my mom that Erekle's grandmother got seriously ill, and she wished to see her daughter and grandchildren. In spite of that, Manana didn't really want to go; she preferred to stay and wasn't even concerned about her mother's health at all until we all heard Erekle's outrageous voice. He was exasperated and yelled at his mother and sister, telling them to pack at once because they had to fly back to Georgia to see his grandma. Erekle was immensely emotional and nervous. He truly loved his grandma. In fact, he was raised by her. She was a very sweet and kind woman. I recall Erekle's words from that day: "If something happens to my grandma, I will never forgive myself and my family for abandoning her." While Erekle kept screaming at his mother and sister, they both carried on packing everything so speedily that within an hour, they were all ready to leave. The entire event occurred so shockingly, unexpectedly, and quickly that I felt as if a wild storm swept my in-laws away from my life forever. As soon as they left the apartment, got into the cabs, and drove off, I was so ecstatic that I screamed, jumped, and danced on the little wooden coffee table with Chiko! Finally, we celebrated our newfound freedom and joy. Since that day, I never saw my in-laws again.

When Erekle arrived back in Istanbul from Georgia, after his grandmother recovered from her illness, my father still hoped that without my in-laws' presence, Erekle would've been different, more attentive, caring, and responsible towards Chiko and me. So my dad asked me to give Erekle a chance to see how everything would develop and turn around this time. In my heart, I already knew that my relationship with Erekle was over, yet before fully closing that chapter, I gave him a chance. Unfortunately, each day my parents were getting more and more discouraged and upset by his neglectful, presumptuous, and ungracious behavior. One day, when Erekle was out, I cleaned the entire closet in my bedroom and I accidently discovered a large amount of cash hidden in one of the drawers in the closet. I didn't know anything about that money until that day. During our relationship, Erekle had never shared any money or discussed finances with me. I closed the drawer without touching anything and didn't say a word to anyone. It was obvious that he got that cash from his father when he went back to Georgia. I was concerned about it, because at age nineteen, he had access to a substantial amount of money which he could spend freely and secretly on anything. My parents and I knew that Erekle helped his father with business, trading, and marketing, but we didn't know the specifics. One afternoon, when Erekle came home, he told me that he had a terrible headache and wanted to go to bed and sleep. He hardly spoke and was disoriented. My parents were not home, only Chiko and I. The next day, he repeated the same—came home early, looked confused, he slurred his words, and his eyes were closing. I got scared and asked if he was alright. He didn't say anything but just went straight to the bedroom and passed out on the bed where he slept until the next morning. I didn't want to say anything to my parents yet; first, I wanted to find out what was happening with him. The following morning, I spoke with him and told him all of the details about how he looked the day before and asked what was going on with him. His facial expression was as if I was out of my mind. He said that he just had a migraine headache, that was all, and arrogantly walked out of the room. Since then, every other day, he would come home in the early afternoon, intoxicated, and then go to bed right away. My dad was mostly out (he worked long hours); therefore, he never saw Erekle under the influence. On the contrary, my mom noticed it and she was disturbed by his actions and state of being. I was under the impression that he was drinking, but then I realized that I never detected the smell of alcohol on his breath. And many times, I saw him passed out on the bed with drool pouring from his mouth. Ultimately, I was sure that he was taking drugs and as I regularly began counting the cash, which he secretly kept in one of the closet's drawers, I found out that a lot of money was missing on a daily basis. As a result, this incident was the culmination of my marriage. I plucked up the courage and told him firmly that I wanted a divorce, so he needed to pack his belongings and leave the house as soon as possible. That was the day I finally stood up to him. I no longer wanted him to be a part of my and my son's life. He wasn't expecting that statement from me, which of course, offended and humiliated him. He swore and verbally abused me, then said that all the girls were crazy about him and they all loved him, it was me who would regret all of this. After that, he angrily went to the bedroom and began packing. He had so much pride within himself that he hated to be rejected. My parents were there for me and they fully supported my final resolution. Once Erekle walked out of Chiko's and my life, I solidly and completely closed that chapter without ever looking back.

❧

I haven't had a chance until now to talk about my brother, Lasha, who wasn't with us during this tumultuous time. In 1994, a few months before my parents moved to Turkey, my brother moved to Worcester, Massachusetts, USA. He got accepted at Clark University, to get a degree in government and international relations. He was a very determined and committed student and my father worked exceedingly hard to financially support him. When my brother moved to the US, he often called Erekle and me in Israel and shared with us the activities about his life as a student, his challenges and fun that he was having. At the same time, he loved to hear our stories about how our little boy, Chiko, was growing up in Ashdod. Since my brother was very fond of Erekle and genuinely loved him, I didn't want to tell him every little detail about what happened between us so as not to break my brother's heart or disappoint him. Besides, Lasha has always been a very protective, loving, and caring brother and I surely didn't want him to retaliate against Erekle because of me. However, I needed to tell him something about what caused our separation so when I spoke with him over the phone after Erekle's departure, I briefly told him about Erekle's parents and their unhealthy, selfish, and manipulative control over their son, which awfully affected our relationship. Furthermore, I said that Erekle started taking drugs and became very aggressive, irresponsible, and careless towards me and his son and it was unbearable to stay with him any longer and raise Chiko in a harmful environment. Nevertheless, my brother was hurt and saddened from the news, though he was happy that Chiko and I were with my parents, protected and safe. He completely backed my decision and stood by my side. More than two decades later, this will be the first time for my brother to find more truth and nearly all of the details about my relationship with Erekle and his family through this book. I hope he will understand why I didn't want to share this painful experience with him before, because *I love him so much.*

15

A NEW CHAPTER OF MY LIFE
ISTANBUL, TURKEY (1995)

After my separation with Erekle, life in Istanbul took a hundred-and-eighty-degree turn. I was grateful for having freedom and peace, and primarily for having my loved ones around me. My parents offered me their unconditional support and help with Chiko not only physically and emotionally but financially, too. They were prepared to take full responsibility of Chiko and to raise him as if he was their own son. They promised that they would do their best to make sure that Chiko never felt a lack of anything and, most of all, that his life would be filled with love, kindness, and compassion. My father even told me not to ask anything from Erekle and his family. He said, "If they are willing to do something for Chiko, let them do it freely, from their heart, without any demand or pressure. Don't you worry, as long as I'm here, alive, you and Chiko will be protected and taken care of." My dad wasn't just a good father to me, he was greater and bigger than that. He was, and still is, the most trustworthy, selfless, and generous man I've ever known. *Whatever he says, no matter what, he always does it.* His presence in my life has always made me feel strong, like the lyrics of "You Raise Me Up," one of my favorite songs, are:

> *You raise me up, so I can stand on mountains*
> *You raise me up, to walk on stormy seas*
> *I am strong, when I am on your shoulders*
> *You raise me up to more than I can be . . .*
> —Brendan Graham

However, not once did Erekle and his family pay for child support, nor did they ever ask how Chiko was doing. Nevertheless, my parents wanted me to go to college and get a higher education so that one day, I could get a decent job and take care of myself and my son. For me, having total freedom from everything, not being the only person responsible for my own child, and having no other duties but school and studying were all a miracle. I was truly fortunate to have my mom and dad as my parents. I wanted to fly, sing, dance, and laugh again.

∽

When I was in school in Georgia, I had a dream to learn English, but at the time I was unable to grasp and comprehend this language. I found it extremely difficult and complicated. At one point, I thought I would never be able to learn English, yet I didn't give up on it. Now, I want to share with you who really inspired me to learn English. It was 1989 or 1990 (I don't recall the exact time or year) but it was still during the communist regime in Georgia. It was one of the evenings when my parents were sitting in the living room and watching *Vremya* (Time), the main evening newscast in Russia. It was airing on Program One of the Central Television of the USSR.[21] As a child, I was never interested in the news, but what caught my full attention that evening was the deep baritone voice of a man on TV who spoke in English while interviewing the General Secretary of the Communist Party of the Soviet Union, Mikhail Gorbachev. Even though an interpreter was translating the questions into Russian and the entire news segment was very brief, I was still able to hear a few lines by a middle-aged American interviewer, whose spoken English was so striking and memorable that, in that moment, I had a huge desire to learn to talk in English fluently and to be able to completely understand that outstanding talk show host. The name of that man was Larry King, who hosted the nightly interview television show *Larry King Live* on CNN.

In order to pursue my dreams, I decided to find a college in Turkey that had all English programs and courses. After a thorough search, one day, my father came home from work and informed me that he found a college in Istanbul that had just opened up in 1995 and was accepting local as well as international students. Additionally, it had a variety of other programs, which were based on the English language. The name of the college was Beykent Institute of

Higher Education (BIEK), which operated in cooperation with Liverpool John Moores University (LJMU). BIEK had faculty that specialized in communication and mass media studies, and that was the direction in which I was interested and wanted to follow. First, I began as a preparatory student, since I was at zero level in English, and then it was up to me how fast I could move up to the next level and so on. I can never forget those precious days—getting up early in the morning, walking ten to fifteen minutes to the bus station, and waiting for a school bus to take me to college, which took an hour and a half for just a one-way drive. I used to get car-sick all the time, and I still do if I sit back in the passenger's seat. So, for that reason, I was worried about getting into the bus with the new students and being embarrassed in front of them. But I was lucky that the front seat was available for me, which made me feel relieved. Yet beyond everything, the school bus was filled up with amazing local students, whose kindness, humor, friendship, and hospitality created the most engaging and enjoyable atmosphere in the bus. Every day, being among those students was a blessing for me, since all of those awesome, fun youths in the bus tried to teach me Turkish and they laughed a lot at my pronunciation. I found Turkish easier than other languages. I loved learning it and no matter how bad or funny my pronunciation was, I kept repeating and practicing the Turkish words.

I can proudly write about my first year at BIEK and LJMU; every single educator that I came across was exceptionally supportive, professional, and encouraging. They were there for all students. My English instructor was

Turkish; she was a very devoted and driven teacher and had a beautiful name as well, which was Gamze (it means "dimple on cheek" in Turkish). She was my first and best English-language teacher, who ultimately was able to make English understandable and clear to me. She gave me confidence and hope that I could learn anything if I believed in it and put my effort into it.

School became my number one priority. I began appreciating everything that I was given or experiencing, and most significantly, I was grateful for my parents for allowing me to follow my dreams. After going through a tumultuous and agonizing marriage, I realized how lucky I was to be home, and healthy, with my loving family. I recognized that I should never take anything for granted, because if I didn't have my parents then, I don't know what would have happened to Chiko and me. I have continued giving thanks to my family and others and remain grateful for my life. Each day, our lives in Istanbul were turning more and more joyful and magical. I was studying intensely. I put all of my time and effort into my schoolwork and my English was improving dramatically. My central focus was nothing but learning and growing. A year later, after passing the TOEFL test (Test of English as a Foreign Language, a standardized test), I was delighted that I could move up and get into a foundation course, a program that was going to prepare me for an undergraduate degree at a university. While I was diligently studying and doing well at college, my father's business in Turkey had astonishingly begun growing and blooming. During the first year after my parents moved to Istanbul, my father faced many challenges and therefore that year was full of financial struggles as he attempted to get his company off the ground. Fortunately, the second year when we were united and exulted, his company was doing unbelievably well. My father was able to continue to pay my brother's tuition in the US, and surprisingly, he offered me an opportunity to pursue my higher education in England. He acknowledged my commitment and hard work and wanted to support me all the way so that I could accomplish my goals and fulfill my dreams. If anyone had told me two years earlier (when I was in Israel with my ex-husband and ex-in-laws) that one day I would study in England, I would've responded, "Only in my dreams." I would have never believed then that it would have been possible. At times, you don't even grasp the impact a person had on you until into the future, when you look back and become aware that one person was vital in encouraging and guiding you at just the right time. My ex-father-in-law's friend, Tatiana, was that person, who showed up in my life very fleetingly, performing random acts of kindness that touched me, and her words about women's education imprinted on my mind forever. Since then, those visualizations and intentions of receiving education truly made my dream come true. Currently, I believe one million percent that anything in this life is possible, and anything is achievable, as long as you don't limit yourself. The more you envision, the further you can get with good intentions, focus, patience, and hard work.

16

MY STUDENT YEARS
ENGLAND (1997-2000)

In the first week of January 1997, I transferred from BIEK and LJMU foundation courses to Bellerbys College in Brighton, England, where I continued a foundation program that enabled international students to enter UK universities at a first-year undergraduate level. Bellerbys College was, and still is, an international boarding school in the UK. During my second year in Istanbul after passing the TOEFL test, I got into a foundation program and I thought my English was good. I was getting more and more confident about learning English; however, as soon as I arrived at Bellerbys College and met with other students and teachers, I was completely lost because most of those students spoke English as if it was their first language. The classes also were awfully difficult and I couldn't understand my fellow students very well. Everyone was speaking way too fast. I was shy and mostly quiet both inside and outside the classes so I patiently listened to others and tried to learn from them. I took government, politics, and sociology classes at college and they sounded to me like other foreign languages. The first couple of months I was failing. My lecturers and teachers were very concerned about me being able to get into any university in London that year, since I was the weakest student in my classes according to their assessment. Although I knew that I was at a very low level and needed a colossal amount of work to reach the qualifying percentage (grades) in the exams in order for me to get into one of the universities in London, I was still very positive and determined. Let me be honest with you; in Georgia, I was a very good student, not because I was exceptionally clever, talented, or special, but because I was working extremely hard. I was a very slow learner, unlike my brother. He could finish all of his homework literally in twenty to twenty-five minutes and I would be studying for hours and hours until very late in the evening. That's how I was, and I am not ashamed of that, since I was getting very good grades in school. And not only that, but I also still remember many things I learned in my school years. Additionally, during my time at ulpan and then at BIEK and LJMU, I had discovered a new method and style of learning, which helped me to learn Hebrew and English more effectively and faster than I used to learn things at school in Georgia. The secret tool that I started using since then is if I want to learn something new, distinct, or challenging, I always write it down several times and read it aloud to myself. By writing, I could remember not only the words but, at the same time, I learned and remembered the order and structure of the sentences and grammar, which was so crucial. And by reading everything out loud, it helped me to practice pronunciation and diction. However, at Bellerbys College, I created my own strategy to study and prepare for the exams. In order to get into a university, I needed sixty to sixty-five percentage points in each class, which was a grade B+. Receiving a B or B+ in three months was highly demanding but achievable for me if I followed my plan and trusted it fully. Our educators at college would give us an extra credit if we used additional information, statistics, and facts that were not taught from the college textbooks. So, I had enough data to accomplish my mission. As a result, I began gathering some books about the prime ministers of the United Kingdom for my government and politics class and proceeded with that. Due to my poor vocabulary, I was incapable of understanding almost every other word in those books; however, my dictionaries, which I always carried with me wherever I went, helped me tremendously. I had an English–Russian dictionary, since I couldn't obtain an English–Georgian dictionary at that time. So, if I couldn't grasp the word in Russian, I also had a Russian–Georgian dictionary, and even a Georgian–Georgian dictionary. There were some specific words in politics that I needed to interpret from Georgian to Georgian too. Just reading one page in the book and demystifying every part of it usually took me hours, as I endlessly kept translating tons of words from one language into another and then another while studying them. That's how zealous I was to learn English; that was my true calling.

My lecturers for politics and sociology used to return homework to the students after they revised and corrected everyone's assignments and essays. So, every time I got my edited papers back, I studied each revision in depth by re-writing it countless times until I knew everything meticulously. That technique and practice helped me to enhance my vocabulary and improve my writing skills. On top of that, my writing became more consistent, and easy to decipher. Time was running out. I only had around twenty-five days left before the final exams and I was certain that I needed to concentrate twenty-four by seven on my studies. I recall that those twenty-five days were enormously exhausting. I wanted nothing else but to pass my exams and get into a university in London.

I intended to study multimedia journalism (broadcast), which was the most interesting and fascinating course to me. I love people and especially during my student years in England, I loved talking and listening to the diversity of people there, learning about their various cultures and ethnicities, and hearing some incredible and life-changing stories. I was always curious and drawn to hear stories from the elderly because they had so much to share and I was hungry to learn and grow. In addition, since my childhood, I loved the camera, holding a microphone, performing on stage, and dancing. But my main passion was writing and reciting poems and connecting with the audience. Therefore, I had no doubt that, in those years, mass media was the right path for me to follow.

In June 1997, after receiving my exam results, I couldn't believe what I saw on my final papers. In government and politics, I received an A+; in Sociology, my grade was a solid A; and my final English grade was a B! You can imagine now how I felt. At that moment, I was the happiest person in the world! Though I was extremely contented, I could hardly express my ecstatic feelings because I was overly exhausted and worn out. I'm not writing this to brag about myself and my grades but I am sharing with you one of the most exciting and unforgettable experiences in my life *for one reason only.* If someone like me, who was a less- than-average student, who had no special skills or talent, and who was a very slow learner, could accomplish results like that then I believe more than one hundred percent that *anyone* can achieve their desired goals if they believe in themselves, work hard, and never give up.

The following three years I studied multimedia journalism at the University of Westminster and lived in Harrow, a lively town very close to the university. My entire focus was on my classwork, homework, learning, and successful graduation from the university. Even though I had so many amazing friends—all different nationalities at college and university—and I loved hanging out and spending time with them, I never once dated anyone. I refused invitations from every guy who asked me out. The pain from the past, which I had buried deep within me was still there and I just didn't want to acknowledge or accept it. I thought every guy would be just like Erekle and that they would disappoint, hurt, and take advantage of me, and that scared me. So, I was never interested in anybody. I became very distant and cold where boys were concerned and if anyone still tried to pursue me, I used to lie to them by saying that I had a boyfriend back in my native country whom I loved so much and couldn't betray. My only purpose in London was to acquire my education, then go back to Georgia to pursue my career, and become financially independent and secure. However, before attaining all of that, my third and final year at the University of Westminster began with shocking news.

The news that I received from Georgia was horrifying. I found out that Erekle was shot and killed in Tbilisi. I still don't know the real cause of that deadly shooting; however, that news shattered me. For two weeks, I stayed home, away from everyone. I didn't want to see my lecturers, fellow students, or friends. I longed for solitude and peace as I grieved for Erekle. He was only twenty-four years old then. He had his entire life ahead of him but it ended in 1999. He left two beautiful children with us—Chiko, who was five years old, and a baby girl, from his second marriage, who wasn't even a year old when he died. During those two weeks of grieving, I was only reminiscing about the extraordinarily magical days and months we had before our marriage. I felt that was what Erekle wanted me to remember—just the sweet moments and loving days we shared together, which truly ignited the spark in my heart. I was overly sad because his choice to follow the path of addiction to drugs and money was what ultimately killed him.

Surely, the final year at Westminster was bittersweet for me. I was happy and grateful for graduating from the

University and for being able to go back to Georgia and live with my son and family again. But, on the contrary, I was so sorrowful for the loss of my son's father. My parents had moved back to Georgia with Chiko a few months after I left Turkey to move to England. My father transferred his business to Georgia in 1997 and continued working with his business partners in Tbilisi. My family was thrilled and couldn't wait to finally have me back after my graduation. I was ecstatic to be returning home.

17

REUNITING WITH MY FAMILY
AND
MY FIRST JOB
TBILISI, GEORGIA (2000)

During my student years in England, I had a hard time being without Chiko. Even though I was able to visit my family in Georgia for holidays, when I returned to school, I still used to get very emotional, especially when I spoke with my son over the phone; I was missing him terribly. However, I often reminded myself that being away from my child and family was temporary, and the knowledge and skills that I was acquiring in England were priceless. The end of academic year of 2000 arrived fast, and I was exhilarated to be reconciled with my family back in Georgia.

As soon as I moved back home, I began looking for an internship job at television stations. I was enthusiastic about finding an internship or volunteer work specifically at Rustavi 2, which is a Georgian free-to-air television channel based in Tbilisi and was founded in the town of Rustavi in 1994.[22] Rustavi 2 had professional, competent, tough, and brave journalists and reporters and I had an aspiration to be a part of their team. I was geared up to take any opportunity that was available at the station. Fortunately, in the fall of 2000, I started some volunteer work with them and became an assistant to one of the TV show producers at the station. The period of 2000–2001 at Rustavi 2 was purely a year of learning and growing for me. I was passionately doing all of my volunteer work and was utterly committed to every task I was given. After a year and half, I still wasn't an employee of Rustavi 2. Despite that, my obstinate determination kept me moving forward. I persistently continued my volunteer job, stayed positive and patient, and never gave up on it. I fervently kept pursuing my dreams and simultaneously kept learning from everyone at the station.

In the beginning of 2002, Rustavi 2 gave me an opportunity and the news department trained me for eight months for a weather presenter's position for the morning show. In those years in Georgia, we didn't need to have a degree in atmospheric sciences (meteorology) or in a related field to become a weather reporter. Every single morning, Rustavi 2's news department used to receive the weather forecast from the city's meteorological center, which was already translated into understandable content. However, a weather presenter's job was to report whatever forecasts she or he obtained that particular morning. I practiced intensely every day in the newsroom and learned how to use the teleprompter. I was so driven and passionate to learn everything about this job, but I particularly loved the weather. Because of the daily dynamic weather changes, I knew that I would be constantly learning new things. And for that, I was so grateful for the opportunity.

In September of 2002, I became a full-time employee of Rustavi 2 and began reporting the weather for the morning show, not from the news studio, but outdoors. My major setting was at Turtle Lake, which was located on the wooded northern slope of Mount Mtatsminda at an elevation of 686.7 m above sea level.[23] It was named Turtle Lake because of the abundance of turtles in the area. As a weather reporter, I couldn't wish for any better spot than a small, graceful lake that was surrounded by beautiful nature.

I loved outside broadcasts. Although I didn't have a monitor or autocue, the weather report that was provided by the meteorological center every morning was clear, easy to read and pass on to the audience. Still, I needed to remember things. I frequently used to promote various products live on TV before forecasting the weather and I had to memorize different scripts early in the mornings. Sometimes there were days when the weather forecast was wrong, but you really can't blame anyone for that because it's forecasting, and anybody who forecasts any type of data knows that things can go wrong from time to time. Every single day was distinctive, firstly because I was outside, surrounded by nature; and secondly, the weather changed every day. No matter what, I never missed a day of work, even during those freezing winter mornings when the temperatures dropped so low—sometimes to minus five or six degrees Celsius. I remember my chin and jaw were occasionally so frozen that I had a hard time opening my mouth and speaking properly. I still enjoyed every part of it because I *loved* my job, and I was the happiest person to get up so early in the morning and to prepare myself for work, even when we were without power and running water. I used to do my makeup by candlelight and washed myself with stored water from the night before. In those years, Georgia was still facing a wide range of social and economic dilemmas. Mostly every night, the power and water were cut off until the next morning, around 7:00 a.m., and sometimes throughout the day, too. In spite of that, I stayed optimistic and every morning I yearned to bring positive energy and vibes to the audience. Irrespective of what the weather was each morning—whether it was rainfall or snowfall or storm or freezing cold—every day was a new day and a new beginning of life and that's what mattered the most. I tried to encourage the viewers to enjoy each day as it was. Moreover, in my weather report, I incorporated short stories that were relatable to the weather and nature and, usually, I used to interview people who were regular visitors to Turtle Lake. I wanted to make the weather report fun and informative for everyone, especially for the kids, since they were the ones who were most adversely affected by the poor socioeconomic conditions within the country. So, each morning, I collected enjoyable and engaging stories that were about animals, nature, kids, and climate, and from time to time, I changed the location settings and broadcasted the weather from the places that were exciting for the kids. For example, one day I reported the weather from the zoo and featured some animals, describing how they were getting ready for the day during their morning routine. Another broadcast that I did was about a little painted turtle that was frozen solid in Turtle Lake for several weeks and then came back to life. Sometimes, I recited poems that were suitable for the weather that day and on some occasions, I interviewed the children who used to get up early in the morning and, before going to school, come with their parents to Turtle Lake to exercise. My intention was to motivate and encourage all the children in Georgia to embrace healthy living. All of those amazing reports and broadcasts would've been impossible if I didn't have an outstanding team and support crew. I tremendously enjoyed working with all of my colleagues in front of the camera, as well as with those behind the scenes. I hugely respected all of my camera operators who were there with me, specifically in those freezing mornings, who genuinely supported me with every single task, and helped and cheered me up when things went wrong. On one drizzly morning, I was standing on a steep slope, because the view behind me was magnificent and that's where I wanted to stand during my weather report. The camera was set up and I was getting ready for my broadcast. I was checking my hair and had only a couple of minutes before going live, but suddenly I fell down the steep and slippery slope and disappeared from my spot. The camera crews got so scared, and they rushed to see if I was OK. Luckily, I wasn't hurt, and I climbed up and still zestfully announced the weather that morning. Incidents like that happen all the time; once I had even dropped a wireless microphone into Turtle Lake just a few seconds prior to one of my reports and my courageous camera guys retrieved it before it was swallowed by the lake. Those mornings and days were unforgettable and unrepeatable; therefore, I am thankful for having lived through those times as they created the incredible memories that are so meaningful and dear to me. Not only was I doing something that I loved so much, but because my life was about to take another dramatic turn.

One of the early mornings, when I was getting ready for my weather report, I was looking for someone to interview at Turtle Lake. Suddenly, I saw a couple of guys jogging and they were approaching the spot where I was standing with my cameraman. So, I decided to stop them both and ask a simple question about how weather affected their mood or if it did at all. One of them just passed me quickly and didn't want to stop, but the other one paused and froze at the same time. He didn't say a word; he just stared at me and as I laid my eyes on him, we both kept staring into each other's eyes and the silence remained so fleeting but deep. That morning was peaceful and chilly, but pleasant. The sun was shining and embracing us; we stood quietly for a few seconds and that was a magical morning for both of us. His name was Giorgi (George) and since that day, he persistently kept coming every morning to Turtle Lake to see me there, and I was anxiously looking forward to seeing him too. Since my separation from Erekle in 1995, for almost eight years I hadn't had any relationship with any man. I wasn't interested in anyone until that enchanting morning when I met Giorgi and I knew he was the one I wanted to date.

18

GIORGI'S AND MY JOURNEY TOGETHER
TBILISI, GEORGIA (2002-2005)

Giorgi's and my relationship began unexpectedly and marvelously. Being around him was so easy and comfortable. He was tall, tanned, not overly muscular but lean, with dark blonde hair and gleaming, hazel eyes. He was an attractive young man. In addition to that, he was a very loving, thoughtful, kind, and generous person and an extraordinary artist. Giorgi had a mixed cultural background—his father was one hundred percent Georgian but his mother was originally from Siberia, Russia, and moved to Georgia when she married Giorgi's father. Giorgi came from an educated and humble family. His father, Vaja, had an engineering degree, and he was mainly involved in construction and design of apartment buildings. By the time I met Giorgi, his father was already retired but he was engaged in another activity—farming. Nadia, Giorgi's mother, was retired as well. She was a very sweet, simple, and lovely woman, and an amazing cook. Nadia used to make the best Russian pelmeni (dumplings of Russian cuisine) and homemade fruit juice (kompot). Whenever I visited them, she specially treated me to those rich, delicious culinary specialties that I enjoyed greatly. Giorgi also had a younger brother, Alexander, whom he loved and cared for so much. Under any circumstance, Giorgi was always there for his family; he was an extraordinarily loving and responsible son. Whenever his mom was sick and unable to do the house chores, Giorgi would shop, cook, and clean for his parents; by the way, he was also an incredible cook, like his mother.

Giorgi was a very creative and talented person, who could design, make, and build anything with his gifted hands. He also drew and painted beautiful pieces of art. Every morning, Giorgi would come to Turtle Lake to exercise, then he went back home to change. But before he went to work, it was our tradition to have breakfast together after my weather reports. We even had our favorite cozy café place, which had the most flavorful homemade pastries and desserts. Spending time with Giorgi was peaceful and effortless, downright opposite from Erekle. Perhaps that's what attracted me to him—his calmness and simplicity. Plus, I highly valued his integrity and equality in our relationship. With Giorgi, I felt heard and supported in all the things I did, as well as appreciated. Above all, I felt free to be myself and I was able to ask for anything I wanted. Somehow, I compared Giorgi to my beloved maternal grandfather, since he was so artistic and resourceful and could fix or build anything with his talented hands, just like my grandfather used to do.

Giorgi and I became inseparable. Anywhere I went, he unexpectedly would show up and surprise me. He always wanted to be not only with me but with Chiko, too. He loved spending quality time with Chiko. He was so tender, loving, and considerate towards my son, which was crucial for me. Chiko was just eight years old, and he loved being around Giorgi; he felt safe and free with him. So, after seven months of dating, Giorgi and I spontaneously decided to get married and start a family together. Some of my family members and friends didn't approve of my decision, but despite that, they accepted my decision without interfering. The reason why they didn't favor my choice was that they were worried about Giorgi's past experiences.

When I met Giorgi, he was thirty-one years old. He was open and honest with me and told me that he suffered from drug and alcohol addiction for a long time since his youth until his mid-twenties. When I met him, he had already been drug-free for several years and he never experienced a recurrence of his drug use disorder during those years. Regarding alcohol, he said he only drank socially when he was out with his friends and he tried to control his drinking then, too. Sobriety was a high priority for him. He wanted to cultivate other goals in his life and create a happier and healthier lifestyle for himself. After meeting me, he was more determined to follow his plans and to limit alcohol consumption as well. He knew that I had never taken drugs, didn't smoke, and wasn't a big fan of alcohol either. I used to drink socially when I was out with my friends too, but very little. While we were dating, during those seven months, he avoided drinking or drank just a little, like me. Only once I recall that he had exceeded his limit at his friend's house, where there was a small party and he kept consuming alcohol, which made me very uncomfortable. I told him that I wanted to leave and without any problem, he promptly said goodbye to everyone, and we left his friend's house peacefully. Although, when we got outside, he could barely walk. He lost his balance and fell down on the ground, then started throwing up; he was a mess. The next day, I spoke with him earnestly and told him that I couldn't stay in this relationship if he continued drinking like that, regardless of his exceptionally loving personality. His response was that if I gave him an opportunity and established a family with him, he promised that he would stop drinking. I truly believed in him and his words. I didn't realize then how addicted he was to alcohol. I *ignored it* and focused on the good traits, which in fact drew me towards him—his gentleness and easiness, benevolence and unselfishness. Perhaps those were the qualities that I was seeking in a man, which were so valuable to me. After the traumatic and terrifying experience with my ex-husband, I had a desire to be with someone with whom I could be fearless, carefree, and myself.

As a result, at the end of May 2003, Giorgi and I got married. We just had a very small gathering, nothing formal, with our family members and a few close friends. We didn't want to have a large ceremony or party; we were both content with everything we had. Besides, I was aware of Giorgi's financial state. He earned a very low wage at the company he worked for, and it was hardly enough for a person to sustain him- or herself. Despite that, I never judged

Giorgi based on his financial status and never expected *material things* from him. But I recognized his unlimited potential and the incredible gifts that he had, and I was confident that he could accomplish anything if he put his effort and mind to it. He was a very good man and that's what mattered to me the most. I loved his soul and courageous heart. Indeed, financially, I was very fortunate and secure because of my parents' ongoing support. Aside from that, I had a full-time job at Rustavi 2, although my salary too was very low and not enough to support my family. But I believed that Giorgi and I together, with our creativity, willingness, and common goals, could build a solid foundation on which we would establish a joyful, successful, and healthy life. After our marriage, we moved into the house that I grew up in. My father had gifted it to me and only my grandmother lived in it at the time. My grandmother was delighted to have Giorgi and me living with her. She was in her nineties then but she was a very strong and healthy woman.

Once Giorgi and I began our life together, we both were on the same page and didn't plan to have a child right away. First, we wanted to make sure that we were financially secure and independent and were not relying on anyone else. We even used contraceptives so I couldn't get pregnant. In addition to that, we were both young; I was twenty-six and already had a grown-up child and Giorgi was in his early thirties. So, neither of us was in a rush to have a child. Having said that, I still accidentally and surprisingly got pregnant and of course, without question, we merrily decided to keep the baby.

I can proudly say that Giorgi was the most caring, patient, and loving husband during my pregnancy. He would do anything for me. Due to severe morning sickness in my early pregnancy, almost every night Giorgi would cook, clean, and prepare things for the next morning so that I would not have to worry about cooking or doing anything the following day. I felt so safe and relaxed around him all of the time until one day, four and a half months after our marriage, he came home late in the evening and was absolutely roaring drunk. He barely spoke and hardly stood on his feet. I didn't say a word; it would have been pointless. I was just glad that he came home safe, so I let him be. He immediately went to the bathroom, threw up, and spent all night on the bathroom floor. Needless to say, the next day, I gently reminded him of his promise that he would quit drinking if we established a family together; yet he broke his promise, and I was very disappointed in him. He barely remembered anything, albeit he was very remorseful and sorry about that incident and gave me his word that he wouldn't drink like that anymore. The following three months continued as he promised, that is, he was sober. Then, another incident arose, which was even worse. I don't recall exactly, but I believe I was about eight months pregnant. One evening, Giorgi came home with his friend, who was sober, but Giorgi was highly intoxicated, so much so that he hardly could stand on his feet. He slurred and told me to go with them to one of their friends' house, where there was an outdoor party. I politely replied to both that I wasn't feeling well and had no desire to go anywhere. Giorgi insisted, which annoyed me and made me very uncomfortable in front of his friend. It thus got to the point where I stood aloof from them and, with my irritated voice, I said that I wasn't going anywhere and walked out of the room angrily. Giorgi's friend promptly left the house after my unfriendly response. Afterwards, Giorgi came into the kitchen, where I was, angrily opened the kitchen utensil drawer, took out a sharp knife, and was ready to stab himself in the stomach. For a second, I was stunned and was unable to react because that kind of behavior from Giorgi was beyond shocking. He was so drunk and didn't realize what he was doing. He looked mad and kept mumbling, "I will hurt myself with this knife, I will hit it into my stomach." His outrageous demeanor convinced me that he could do anything in that moment; luckily, he didn't threaten me. He didn't want to hurt me, just himself. Therefore, with a loving voice, I gently started to calm him down and I begged him to put the knife back in the drawer and not to injure himself. Surprisingly, he listened to me and placed the knife back in the drawer, then walked out of the kitchen straight to the family room, where he spent all night sleeping on the couch.

That night, I was ruminating on my past experiences with Erekle, who verbally abused and threatened me all the time. On the contrary, Giorgi had never threatened or abused me but he was capable of physically harming himself, which alarmed me. However, what scared me the most was that if Giorgi continued to drink like that, while he might physically hurt himself, he could also cause emotional and psychological pain to me and our baby. He needed help, but I didn't know how to help him. Although I wasn't as young as I was in my first marriage, I still had no knowledge or experience about many things. Besides, I didn't want to disclose any of my personal issues and problems with anyone, particularly with my parents. Since my parents suffered and worried enough about my first marriage and they also were raising my son, Chiko, I didn't want to cause more distress to them. Consequently, I remained silent and chose to take care of these personal matters by myself.

The day after that terrifying event, I had a serious and calm discussion with Giorgi about his addiction to alcohol and I pointed out specifically how it was harming him, me, our unborn baby, and our life together. What I actually noticed while I was speaking with him was that he didn't want to hear what transpired the night before. He wasn't inclined to accept that he had a severe problem with drinking and needed some help. The only thing he said was that he would never hurt or harm me or our baby and apologized for creating any trouble. He said once more that it wouldn't happen again, and then he changed the topic. I chose not to linger on the same topic either.

Soon after our baby boy, Luka, was born in February 2004, Giorgi lost his job. He was laid off and his job loss considerably affected him. Alternatively, I was really OK with that. I didn't worry about it because, in reality, his salary was too low and not sufficient to sustain a family anyway. Hence, I believed there was a reason why that occurred. Fortunately, we didn't need to pay monthly mortgage, yet we had some utility bills and other expenses which, thankfully, were covered by my parents. Giorgi had his pride and felt ashamed for not being able to provide. Although his income at the company he had worked for was low, it still used to make him feel better because he knew that he contributed something to his family. I was very supportive and understanding. I never made Giorgi feel that he lived in *my* house and not in *his*, or that my family continually paid all of our bills. That was never a discussion between us. Since I met Giorgi and before I married him, I was aware of his financial background. I knew that he lived with his parents, owned no property, and had a low income, and I still chose him not because of what he had but because of who he was. He had so much potential and talent and if we both started off with whatever we had initially, I believed we could build our fortune together. I stayed very optimistic and came up with an idea to open a small bakery in our house's basement, where we could prepare a few freshly baked recipes such as traditional Georgian cheese bread (Khachapuri), bean bread (Lobiani), and meat and potato piroshki, which were—and still are—very popular in Georgia. If the plan and business turned out well, we could have focused on other recipes as well. Therefore, I considered some key factors that were critical before opening a bakery business. First, I found out that it was legal and that we had all the rights to open a home-based bakery in my area. Second, because I had a big space in my house's basement, I could make all kinds of adjustments for whatever we needed to operate a home bakery effectively. Most importantly, I had someone in mind who could help us and whom I knew since my childhood. She was one of the most skillful bakers and cooks I had ever known, and her name is

Enrico. We call her "Enro" and she is an extraordinarily special lady, not only to my family but also to many people in Georgia. Originally, she is from Akhaltsikhe (literally "new castle"), which is a small and beautiful city in Georgia's southwestern region of Samtskhe–Javakheti.[24] Enro was my parents' closest, dearest, and most loyal friend. She met my parents before my brother and I were born, and since then, they have developed an invaluable and precious friendship. My mom treated her like her own sister. Enro is a single woman who never married. She has devoted her entire life to serve and help others. I call her "the giver" because that's who she is. Since I was a little girl, I recognized that she was consistently open and ready to give as much as she could and share her love with others. She didn't have much and wasn't materially rich, but she was the wealthiest woman in her heart and soul. My brother and I often stayed with Enro when my parents were out of town and we had the most unforgettable days just being with her alone. She was so much fun. She spoiled and allowed us to be free to do anything we wanted. In fact, she used to teach me how to bake cakes, pies, and cookies, particularly when my mom wasn't present because my mother hated the mess we used to create in the kitchen during baking. Enro frequently travelled from Akhaltsikhe to Tbilisi to stay with us and she would often help my mom when we had big events at home. She was the most creative artist in the kitchen. Using only a few simple ingredients, she could turn them into a delightful feast. She was, still is, part of our family. Our love, respect, and appreciation have been mutual and unconditional. It is so true that families are defined not by blood but by love.

When the idea of home bakery business came into my mind, the first person I thought about was obviously Enro. So, I was confident that she would have helped me before we could find someone else whom she could train. To be honest with you, I had never been interested in the food business. That wasn't my niche and I had no clue about how to manage it, though I was willing to learn and acquire the necessary basic knowledge for this unknown field. Beyond everything, I had no fear of failing. Even though I loved my profession and greatly enjoyed working at Rustavi 2 (regardless of my low salary), I allowed myself to try new things because my curiosity had always kept me moving forward, exploring, and accepting new challenges. Additionally, I had a family, was a responsible mother and wife, and had a huge desire to become financially secure and independent. I persistently kept seeking how to create more financial stability so that my husband and I could take care of everything by ourselves. However, what truly propelled me to open a home bakery business was Giorgi, as I didn't want him to get depressed about not having a job. I didn't want him to feel powerless and continually mourn the loss of his job which could have turned him back to drinking. I loved him and strived to convey my sincere support with everything I was able to do. I watched how he looked for other jobs, but unfortunately, he had no success.

When I shared my plan with Giorgi, he totally loved the proposition and was very excited about pursuing this new venture with me. However, I made it very clear at the beginning that I would put in as much time as I could, and I would even ask my family to financially help us to set the plan into motion to bring this project to fruition only if he promised that he would take the responsibility to market our home bakery products after we launched the business. I told him that to get our bakery business off the ground, we wouldn't only need to spread the word and actively engage ourselves within our residential community, but he would need to sell our products at local bakery stores, local events, and other venues. Since I had an infant whom I was nursing at that time, I wouldn't be able to do these types of activities. I didn't want to take any steps unless I was sure that Giorgi was willing to oversee and become accountable for the bakery business thoroughly and wholeheartedly. He sounded very positive and encouraged me to take actions to turn our plan into reality. The first step I made was that I shared our plan with my parents and asked them for their financial help to start our small business. My parents and my brother were always there for me and, in unison, they approved of and supported our project. In about forty-five days, Giorgi and I, with the generous help of Enro, were able to launch our first business from our home. That was a big step for us as a family and we were very lucky that we had Enro with us from the day one. She tirelessly helped us with all of the recipes and graciously trained a young baker for about a month, who eventually replaced her. We developed tasty and attractive products that were well received and liked but there were many other challenges that we faced. Since we couldn't simply display our products on a shelf or advertise in our windows, we needed to ask local bakeries about placing some of our products on their store displays or about purchasing them at wholesale prices. Giorgi also needed to visit local catering companies and other vendors who regularly supplied services for large events and parties, to offer our home-baked goodies for sale. Marketing became one of the most challenging factors in our home-based business, not only because neither of us had experience in promoting or selling products or services, but because at that time, there was no social media—what we now know to be a powerful marketing tool. Despite his efforts, Giorgi's unhealthy mindset affected the business immensely. Anxiety and fear challenged him the most. He worried about not selling all the units that he delivered to the retailers daily. He complained that this was a very competitive business and there were many other well-established baking companies that were more liked and preferred by the vendors. As a result, Giorgi became reluctant in reaching out to new vendors, networking, and creating fresh opportunities. In fact, our small volume of products would sell out in the local stores, during our first month of operation. In spite of that, despair washed over Giorgi and he generated a very negative outlook of not being effective or profitable in our business. Regardless of my optimistic attitude and endless encouragement, I was realistic in knowing that it was just our second month and we were still in the process of learning and expanding our knowledge in a brand-new and unfamiliar field. Clearly it wasn't an easy task, but with positive intentions and an excellent customer service, I believed we could have done well. Having said that, one of the core reasons that really affected our business was Giorgi's continued inability to control his use of alcohol. He thought that consuming alcohol would help him deal with his fears and anxieties. Perhaps it helped him for a short period of time, as it numbed his pain and emotional distress. But that was just temporary. As time was passing, our home bakery was failing; we were incapable of marketing our business constructively due to several causes. Primarily, I was worried about Giorgi's ongoing dependence on alcohol, which was hurting him physically as well as emotionally. He was so overwhelmed and tormented about our home bakery that, at some point, I wished that we never launched this business in the first place. Secondly, I was a caregiver not only for my three-month-old son, Luka, but also for my husband. I was taking up the role of a rescuer and provider for our whole family. Fortunately my older son, Chiko, was still with my parents then, so I knew he was safe and secure and I didn't have to worry about him. Another major reason that we were unable to manage our business productively was that we both rushed our opening within a few weeks. We didn't have a proper business plan that would have covered everything, such as marketing, demographic analysis, and realistic expectations based on our financial investment. We could have planned better; more importantly, neither of us had passion for baking, nor were we ready to take on all aspects of a business. As a result, we both decided to shut down our bakery two and a half months after its launch.

Earlier I specified that I was willing to learn and acquire knowledge in an unfamiliar field and beyond everything, I had no fear of failing. To be more accurate, I'd say *I had no fear of trying.* Many might say that I had no fear of failing or trying because my extraordinary parents were unfailingly always there for me. In addition to covering most all of my family expenses, they paid for all of my financial losses. It's more than a blessing having parents like I have and a brother, who was there for me on all occasions and for my two boys. In spite of that, I would never have considered opening a home bakery business by myself if not for Giorgi. I loved to see my husband happy and I didn't want him to suffer or to feel defeated since he had no job. I thought that this family business would have uplifted his spirit and it would have given structure and purpose to his life. For that reason, I was prepared to endure anything to bring joy and a smile to Giorgi's face.

When we closed down our business, I wasn't angry or upset and I blamed neither Giorgi nor myself for anything, I just told my husband, "If we didn't try, we wouldn't know whether we were able to manage a home bakery or not, so now we both are assured that this business wasn't for us. At least, we learned that, and I genuinely don't want you to worry about the financial loss either." My family never mentioned to us that we owed them anything. I don't think any of our actions soothed Giorgi's pain; on the contrary, it worsened. My family stayed very positive and tried to motivate him constantly, as did I. I honestly didn't know what else to do; I was helpless and I asked myself, *What else would a young person need to be happy when he or she has a loving and responsible wife or husband, healthy children, a beautiful house with no mortgage, and a very caring and supportive family that provides everything?* Giorgi had all of that, and not once did I pressure or offend him about not having a job or contributing to his family. I wanted him to do something that made him feel good, but clearly, not drinking. Inevitably, he started going out with his friends every other night and drinking. Finding free alcohol in Georgia is very easy because wine holds a significant place in every Georgian family and it's a tradition to offer your guests a drink. Sometimes, he would steal a bottle of wine or other types of drinks from my parents' house and hoped that no one would notice. My mom spotted it a few times but stayed silent, as she didn't want to add fuel to the fire. She recognized that Giorgi was struggling and had an alcohol use disorder but she never said a word to me or to him. My mom was always there for me, though she never intervened in any of my relationships; she was certain if I needed her help, ultimately I would ask. My family was determined to help Giorgi to find a job through their social contacts and networking, but he was rejected every time he had a job interview. I tried to reignite his passion for art and I even bought painting canvases of different sizes with all kinds of painting supplies, I hoped it would have given him some incentive and, in fact, he began painting daily just to express his appreciation of my love and thoughtfulness. Sadly, he had no passion for anything else and he was completely lost. Without anger or reproach, many times I attempted to tell him quietly what his drinking was doing to everyone, that it was destroying him and hurting all of us. And I was sure that if I started fighting with him, he would've physically hurt himself. One time, when he came home drunk, I just made a remark that lit his fuse; immediately after, he smashed a big hole in the wall; he almost broke his wrist, his knuckles were bleeding, and then he ran away. I avoided any kind of drama with him and when he was intoxicated, I let him be. Although I profoundly wanted to help my husband, I really didn't know *how*. And Giorgi never acknowledged that he had any problems; he used to tell me that he didn't drink much and didn't need any help, so I shouldn't worry about him.

Giorgi buried lots of inner, unexpressed anger and torment that were stemmed from his past. He was plagued by his past and was continually disheartened by his family. Despite that, he loved and respected his parents and brother. Although Giorgi never shared with me the pain from his past, I sensed that he was suffering. Today, I believe that by marrying me, Giorgi thought that he would have been able to heal his past and move on. But soon after our marriage, he realized that an affliction still existed within him, and it didn't dissipate. What he didn't perceive then was that *no one* can take away or heal our pain but ourselves. The same can be said about myself. I chose Giorgi not only because of his incredible qualities that I fell in love with, but also because he was the complete opposite of my ex-husband. I compared him to Erekle. When Giorgi was sober, he was so easy to be around, and we were equal partners. For that reason, I ignored the other side of him—his addiction problems. My ignorance of this indicates that I was not fully healed from my past affliction either and I was honest neither to myself nor to him. As Marianne Williamson wrote in her excellent book, *A Return to Love: Reflections on the Principles of "A Course in Miracles"*:

> "As temples of healing, relationships are like a trip to the divine physician's office. How can a doctor help us unless we show him our wounds? Our fearful places have to be revealed before they can be healed. *A Course in Miracles* teaches that 'darkness is to be brought to light, and not the other way around.' If a relationship allows us to merely avoid our unhealed places, then we're hiding there, not growing. The universe will not support that."[25]

Giorgi's and my relationship lost its purpose of being. We weren't growing as individuals within our relationship, rather we were hiding there because we were both controlled by our egos and weren't able to show the real truth about ourselves. Thus, we were unable to help or heal one another, because we didn't reveal our wounds to each other. As much as I continued to ask Giorgi to change and stop drinking, he proceeded to drink more. That's how he numbed his emotional distress and masked the excruciating pain that stemmed from his past. He became more and more distanced and alienated from me, our baby, and everyone else. He developed depression, anxiety, and had no enthusiasm for life. His drinking created a lot of tension in our relationship. While I was aware that I was living with an alcoholic who couldn't and wouldn't stop drinking, I still had a little *hope* that one day he would gain enough courage to admit that he had a problem and would be ready to seek treatment.

Luka was about thirteen months old. It was a tranquil evening. My grandma and I were sitting in the family room, singing and playing with Luka and enjoying the evening until the door opened widely and Giorgi entered the room drunk again. He could barely speak. When I looked at him, the first question that I asked was if he drove himself home. He didn't answer me but he was fully focused on Luka. So, after a little pause, I asked him gently where he spent his entire day. That question aggravated him so badly that he angrily grabbed his car key and jacket and, without a comment, rushed out of the room. Within a minute, I heard the car engine fire up, followed by a sudden loud noise. I jumped up from the chair, told my grandma to watch over Luka, and madly ran out to check on Giorgi. When I got outside, I saw that he crashed his car into the electric pole that was standing on the opposite side of our house. Even though the front bumper of the car was badly damaged, the car engine still kept running. Giorgi was OK. He was sitting in his car and he didn't move or step out to check on the car. But as soon as he got a glimpse of me, he pressed the accelerator pedal and drove off fast like a madman. I instantly knew that he intentionally smashed his car into the pole, and I felt a surge of rage. That moment was the last straw that broke our relationship. I recognized that it was time for me to take responsibility for my own self and my children and allow Giorgi to do the same. I truly wished to have a magic wand and cure him from that disease but I knew it was impossible.

Each of us is responsible for our own choices and no one can save or heal us unless we are willing to be saved or healed. "No one saves us but ourselves. No one can and no one may. We ourselves must walk the path."—Buddha

All my good intentions, hopes, or sympathies weren't serving either of us well. I needed to live a better life for myself and my children and Giorgi himself had to *walk the path*. I especially didn't want my son, Luka, to grow up with an alcoholic father and witness how his dad suffered from that addiction, which would have had a serious effect on my son's risk for future alcohol abuse. As a mother, I strived to protect my children, and whether I was doing it the right way or not, I don't know. But raising my children in a healthy, safe, and peaceful environment was my number one priority. As a result, that night, I packed all of Giorgi's belongings, put everything in two big suitcases along with a short farewell letter, and left them out on the front patio. I was so upset that I didn't want to see or talk to him in person. I don't remember the exact words of that letter, but I recall that I wrote something like this: "Giorgi, when you are sober, clean, and happy, as well as when you find a decent job that allows you to take care of yourself, then we can talk. Until then, I neither want to see you, nor do I want you to be around Luka when you are intoxicated." I deliberately wrote in the letter about finding a decent job, not because I needed anything from him, but because I just wanted him to be able to take care of himself. Although I didn't indicate in the letter that I wanted a divorce when I wrote that letter, I was already certain that Giorgi would never ever stop drinking, and this was the end of our marriage. His promises and lies were endless and he had never acknowledged having a disease. If he was willing to seek treatment and asked for my support, I would have been there for him without question, and together we could have sought professional help. To be honest with you, at that time I personally knew nothing about rehab or alcohol treatment programs, and the idea of searching for these types of specialized programs had never crossed my mind. Obviously, when Giorgi found my letter and his two suitcases on the front patio the next day, he was so humiliated and upset that he left without making any verbal or written remark. In fact, our separation and later divorce transpired very peacefully without any major arguments or disagreement as if we both knew deep inside that this was the time for us to part. Giorgi was sorry and tried to come back many times, but when he ultimately understood that I was adamant about my decision, he told me, "I trusted you." What he meant was that I had no compassion and threw him out of my house when he was jobless and in despair. I never intended to cause any pain to Giorgi, but I was also very upset, heartbroken, and disappointed in him, since I trusted and believed his words. Unfortunately, he was unable to follow through on his promises and it was unbearable for me to watch how my husband suffered in his daily life.

$$\approx$$

Now when I look back, I strongly believe there was a reason why Giorgi and I got together; it was meant to happen, and it wasn't my fault nor his that our marriage didn't work out. I was blessed that our marriage gave me one of the most precious gifts—my son, Luka. But there was something else that I needed to learn from that experience, though I didn't know what it was then. In her profoundly moving book *Broken Open: How Difficult Times Can Help Us Grow,* the author, Elizabeth Lesser, talks about the first difficult days of being separated from her husband of fourteen years. She went looking for a psychic, who told her the following:

> "The truth is that, in order to find yourself, you must leave him. This is your quest. And in order for your husband to find himself, he must lose you. Y'all have lessons to learn—lessons that are more important than the marriage itself. The soul comes to earth to learn lessons, not to get married, or stay married, or to take this job or that job.
>
> But if you are to help him on his soul's quest, you will leave him. It is your job—your sacred contract—to free him, and to free yourself.
>
> Only those who love themselves can love others, that only people who claim their own voice can hear the true song of another."
>
> "It is time for you to answer the call of your soul." "It's calling, but you're too scared to listen. You think you know what's import-ant, but you don't. You think it's important to keep things safe, but that's neither here nor there. What's important in this life is to learn the soul lessons."[26]

After reading this passage, I felt as if that psychic was directly speaking to me and made me realize that in both of my marriages, I needed to learn lessons that were more important than the marriage itself. The psychic's words instantly reminded me of how much I endeavored in both relationships with Erekle and Giorgi to create a safe, contented, and harmonious life. I constantly tried to accommodate, serve, please, and make *them* (my exes) happy, since in my relationships I didn't know who *I was* or what I really wanted. I didn't know my own *worth* and *values* and didn't believe that I had a *power* or a *voice* as well as the *courage* to speak the truth. I never thought to ask myself these two simple questions: Who am I? What do I want? I was lost, resentful, and blamed Giorgi along with Erekle for failing in both marriages, since I assumed that I did as much as I could to provide a secure and healthy environment for our children, but they didn't. However, instead of opening up and learning from those two most meaningful experiences in my life, connecting to my innermost self and listening to my inner voice rather than being scared of hearing the truth, I remained unconscious and stuck in my frightened little mind. I was still not ready to follow the path of truth and, therefore, I began to believe that every man that I met would be a disappointment and failure. And in order to protect myself and my boys, I shuttered my heart, built up a wall, and stayed away from men while focusing on my children and career. Elizabeth Lesser writes:

> "So many of the crises we bring upon ourselves are Angels trying to get our attention.

An illness or loss or heartbreak is often a Hideous Damsel, or a Sleeping Giant, or a Strange Angel who wants to help us evolve. In times of upheaval, we have two choices: We can relate to our circumstances as messengers from the deep, or we can shut down, defend our position, and add another layer of protection to the castle wall. If we defend against the Strange Angels, we will become more and more numb to life. We will remain unchanged. If we allow the Angels entry, we will open the door to change and evolution."[27]

In my late twenties, I ignored the signs of truth that were showing up repetitively on my journey. I was unable to go beneath the surface of my frightened mind and connect with my true essence because I wasn't present enough and, thus, I wasn't ready to *open the door to change and evolution.*

19

MOVING ON

TBILISI, GEORGIA (2005)

When I separated from Giorgi, I decided to fully focus on my career and, of course, on my children. Deep inside I was very sad, but externally I was still able to suppress my sorrow so no one would notice it. I was committed to move on and create a better future for myself and my boys.

Being hired as a weather reporter at Rustavi 2 in 2002 was an incredible opportunity for me and I was very grateful for the chance to prove my skills. However, three years later, I wanted to take up more challenges that offered me professional growth as well as increased income. My monthly salary at Rustavi 2 was very low and because of that, I was still completely dependent on my family to help me with both of my children. Apart from this, I had never received any child support from either of my children's fathers. The problem at my work was that the managers and the head of Rustavi 2 were aware that I was from a successful family, so they never considered an increase to my wages, despite recognizing my devotion and hard work. They assumed that I was financially secure and didn't need more income. Because Tbilisi is such a small city, almost everyone knows one another—it's like a big family. You can't hide who you are, who your parents are, how you live or even breathe. In fact, a few times, my mom gave me advice and told me to ask for a raise at work but I never did, since I had heard from some of my co-workers at the station that I was so lucky to have such a fortunate family. They complained that their income at the station wasn't enough to pay their bills and they had no other financial support. That made me feel very uncomfortable and I was embarrassed to ask for a raise. I assumed if I asked for more, it would make me look greedy, irrespective of the amount of effort, time, and love I put into my work. I also didn't receive compensation for the live commercials that I used to do regularly on TV either. Despite this, I consistently attempted to be appreciated and valued for my own efforts. In truth, I was disappointed, but I presumed if the managers didn't consider increasing my wages then I didn't deserve it or wasn't worth it. And I also had a *fear* of losing the job if I asked for more. I carried on being silent, but at the same time, I started looking for other opportunities. I wanted a change. What I was unable to grasp in those days was that I brought those disappointments upon myself, since I didn't have the courage to speak up and ask for what I wanted. My fearful mind had always tried to predict the outcome. I believed that because of my family's financial status, the company wouldn't give me a raise and it would be futile to ask.

Unexpectedly, in August 2005, I got an offer from Imedi Media Holding, which is a private television and radio company in Georgia,[28] to not only be the host of the Georgian cultural show *Alaverdi* that showcased various cultural celebrations and customs, but to also be one of the executive producers of the show. I was so inspired by the opportunity, as it was enormous step up from the weather reporter job to become the host of a Saturday prime-time TV show. Even though the salary was as low as I had at Rustavi 2, I still took the offer because of the opportunity it presented. I was yearning to learn more and trusted that if the show did well, my earnings would increase proportionately. *Alaverdi* became a highly rated show that covered music, stories, cultural dance, poetry, and other Georgian rituals. Fortunately, we signed contracts with two major sponsors before the show aired. In reality, the executives of Imedi Media Holding still weren't content about the success and popularity of the show. Despite the fact that the show had two major sponsors, the TV station wanted more donors and they expected *me* to bring more money to the company. Every other week, I had a meeting with the CFO and other executives of the station regarding this issue; so, if I failed to bring in another major donor that could invest a significant amount of money in *Alaverdi* then they had to cancel the show. The entire first season, I worked under so much pressure, worrying that the show could be canceled at any time if I didn't find more funding. I felt responsible for the entire crew and staff members who worked tirelessly for the show but obtaining more funding for *Alaverdi* became overwhelming. In a nutshell, what I found out later was that the company did have the budget for the show and the only reason they offered me that job was that they expected my family (specifically my brother who, at that time, had a very powerful and influential career) to become a prime investor of the show in order to bring in additional money to the TV station. For that reason, the executives of the company pushed me really hard so that I could make my brother literally pay for my job. I categorically rejected it and after the first season, at the end of December 2005, the show was canceled, and I was out of work.

At Rustavi 2, I was my father's daughter, whereas at Imedi Media Holding, I became my brother's sister. I was heartbroken after I lost my job. I didn't know what to do but what I knew for sure was that I didn't want to be anybody's daughter, sister, or relative at work. I yearned to be appreciated for my own efforts; however, I felt that no one really cared, neither at Rustavi 2 nor at Imedi Media Holding, whether I worked there or not. I had no value or worth and I was no one without my family. For me, having strong men in my life like my father and brother, who loved, cared, and adored my children and me, was a true blessing. They were my male role models and made me stronger. But simultaneously, being tucked safely under their wings and having their constant protection made me powerless to find my own strength to fly. I had the urge to step courageously into my own life and become stronger by myself without them.

So, the fact was that I was out of work and I was a single mom of two boys, and it seemed like I was failing almost in everything I endeavored in Georgia. I blamed others for my failures—my exes and the companies that I worked for. I couldn't sense what *I* was doing wrong. I considered myself a kind, loving, well-educated, and hardworking person, yet what I didn't recognize then was that there was a core piece missing in me. I wasn't true to myself, nor was I able to listen to my inner voice. As a clarification, I didn't accept and value myself and never spoke the truth about what I wanted or how I felt. I didn't want to displease or hurt anyone and, therefore, I tried to remain either quiet or nice towards others. By doing that, I was deceiving and hurting my own self. My soul instead wanted to get my attention so that I could connect with my authentic self and hear the truth. Those experiences that I had encountered wanted to awaken me, but I didn't pay attention what lay beneath, since I was in a deep sleep and powerless to recognize the truth as well as my own worth. Today, what I am certain about is that each and every one of us comes here with unique *gifts* and worth and therefore, now, I believe that it was neither Rustavi 2's nor Imedi Media Holding's fault that I didn't appreciate and value my own self. My personal mantra is now:

> *When you know your own value*
> *Others will value you too.*
> *When you don't know your worth*
> *You give others the power to determine*
> *Your worthiness.*

We all experience loss and pain throughout our lives, and it requires willingness and work to transform our failures and distress into learning and blessings. In order to know what I wanted in every aspect of my life, I first needed to find out who I was, and to do so, I had to continue my journey filled with more challenges and learning. While I was constantly in search of *something* in the past years, I didn't know what it was. My longing for truth caused me to leave my comfortable and sheltered life in Georgia and undergo many tests until I found myself and became the woman I was meant to be.

In February 2006, I felt as if something bigger was calling me to change. I had a strong desire to leave my native country, my family, and friends again and follow my heart's calling. Hence, I made a bold decision and informed my family that I was planning to go to the United States of America, the land of opportunities, to pursue my dreams. I would be taking my younger two-year-old son, Luka, at first to begin a new life without their presence or help. I was aware that I chose an arduous journey, *the road less traveled*, yet I had an ambition and was ready to face any kind of challenges to start from scratch, all over again. I had already been in the USA several times before 2006. My first visit was to the state of Georgia with my mom and brother when I was thirteen years old. For me, as a teenager, who grew up in a communist regime, those two unforgettably magical weeks in Atlanta, Georgia made a significant impact on me. I vividly recall during that unforgettable time, I wished that I lived in the US. Since my childhood, I never was afraid of being in new places, cities, or countries or being surrounded by unfamiliar faces. Quite the opposite. I was invariably curious and loved it when I had no clue what the next moment or day would look like; that's how much I trusted this universe, just believing that everything would be the way it should be.

Obviously, everyone was shocked about the news of my impending move. Frankly, my family and friends thought I was insane. However, my mom told me privately, "You know how much I want to have you near me, but it's your choice how you want to live your life. I never held you back in the past and I won't hold you back now because I love you." My mom's loving words now remind me of the incredibly powerful words of the American poet, Dr. Maya Angelou:

> "I am grateful to have been loved and to be
> loved now and to be able
> to love because that liberates. Love liberates.
> It doesn't just hold—that's
> ego. Love liberates; it doesn't bind."[29]

My mom liberated and supported me to carry on with my own journey to find what I was seeking.

∞

In 2006, I was officially divorced from my husband, Giorgi. Since I didn't have sole custody of our son, I still needed his signed and notarized permission to travel out of the country with Luka. I told Giorgi that I was planning to travel with Luka to the United States for just a couple of weeks. If I told him that I planned to stay in the US longer than two weeks, he would've said no. I lied to him to avoid all kinds of conflicts, but more accurately, I didn't want my son to grow up with an alcoholic father and watch how his dad suffered from addiction. I was determined to raise Luka in a safe, healthy, and peaceful environment like Chiko had, who was growing up with my parents. In fact, I wanted to be far away from Giorgi because every time he visited us, he was either drunk, depressed, or angry and he wasn't doing anything to show us that he was at least trying to change his state of living. On the contrary, he was getting worse, which affected me emotionally and that would have damaged Luka if he grew up in the presence of his father. At that time, I genuinely believed that my decision was reasonable and acceptable.

20

A NEW BEGINNING
CALIFORNIA, USA

In January 2008, two years after Luka and I had already settled down in Northern California, at last, I was able to bring my thirteen-year-old son, Chiko, to the USA. I was the happiest mother, having both of my children with me together and, most of all, I was blessed that I had a full-time job and was able to take care of my boys. However, it was only a few months after Chiko joined me in California when I received tragic news from Georgia that shocked me. My former spouse, Giorgi, accidently fell off of a ladder at the construction site of a friend's house in Tbilisi. Once again, he was drunk. He suffered a traumatic brain injury and died at age thirty-seven. The first thought that I had in my mind after finding out this horrific news was that I couldn't believe that both of my children's fathers were gone. I was appalled and burst into tears but at the same instant, I was racked with guilt of taking Luka far away from his dad. So,

Giorgi left this world without being able to see and embrace his own son. It was three or four months after I left Georgia that Giorgi called my mom and told her that I was a big liar. He was very upset. Frankly, it never was my intent to hurt Giorgi but obviously my actions did. My only wish was to create a better and safer life for our child. I carried that guilt within me all of these years until I confessed the truth to my son, Luka, who is now sixteen years old. Just recently I told him that in order to bring him here to the States, I had lied to his dad. Then I asked him if he thought that I was a bad person because I hurt his father and made him angry at me forever. Luka stood next to my bedroom door quietly while I was speaking and then after a little pause, he looked at me and said with a smile, "No, Mom, you are not a bad person and my dad is not angry at you either. You did the right thing." After that, he immediately fled from the room; he didn't want to hear more about his father. In truth, hearing these words from Luka felt as if Giorgi's spirit spoke to me through my son with love and ultimately freed me from the guilt and shame that I bore for more than a decade.

Luka was about fourteen years old when he first showed curiosity as to why I divorced his father. I told him the cause of our breakup. He listened to me silently and didn't say a word after I finished telling him the truth. He only tucked his head underneath my arm as if he was abashed hearing all of that and then he hugged and kissed me to express his love towards me. Luka is an exceptionally affectionate and loving son, and since I've been raising him by myself all of these years, he has become very protective and close to me. I know that, one day, he needs to leave the nest like his brother, Chiko, did and fly freely into his own life. In fact, Luka has always escaped from conversations about his dad and when I ask him why he doesn't want to talk about his father, his response is, "Mom, I already know everything about my dad, what else do I need to say?" Regardless of that, I frequently keep bringing Giorgi into our discussions and continue reminding my son of what a loving, kind, talented, brave, and wonderful man his father was. Giorgi truly had a beautiful heart and soul; however, the devastating addiction that he suffered from separated him from us for good.

21

Being a full-time mom with a full-time job wasn't easy. However, my mom, who was—and still is—my superhero, used to visit us in California from Georgia and stayed with us for a while to help me out with my boys. While she stayed with me, she minimized my workload, helped me to find the balance between work and my children, and allowed me to breathe freely a little bit. However, when my mother was gone, I was left alone with my boys. But in reality, I wasn't alone because I had my American family—two beautiful ladies, Donna and Margie—who lived very close to me. Donna was Margie's daughter, and she was in her late forties when we became close family friends, whereas Margie was in her mid-seventies. I believe meeting and having these incredibly remarkable women in my and my children's lives was God's will. I called them my American angels. Donna is a single, independent, strong, and very well-established woman. She and her mother lived on their own with their dog Hanley, a

Golden Retriever Lab mix, in a beautiful house in the East Bay region of the San Francisco Bay Area. Hanley was the sweetest and the gentlest dog I had ever met in my life and he was exactly Luka's age. Donna retired early to manage her physical condition as she was afflicted with multiple sclerosis and her mother was there to help her. Despite Donna's physical limitations and use of a wheelchair later in her life, there was hardly anything that she couldn't do, or figure out how to get done. Donna has always acted more like my mom and she has been everything to me—my mentor, mother, teacher, and best friend. Often times, I felt freer and more comfortable to share my personal matters and sorrows with Donna than with my own mom because I didn't want to overwhelm and stress my mother about all of my personal issues. Donna reveled in my success and happiness and she was always there for me to comfort me in my sadness. Margie, on the other hand, treated my children like her own grandchildren and she was ready to do anything for them. She was kind, gentle, and so generous. My sons adored her. She and Chiko used to have frequent long secret chats and they were best friends. Margie cooked, baked, played, and told stories to my boys and shared her hugs and laughter with them. She was a remarkable and wise woman, who planted so much love in our hearts, and therefore, losing her in 2012 after her fierce struggle with cancer for several months was awfully painful for all of us. No matter where you are or where you come from, if you open your heart to love and to be loved, you will meet people in every part of this world who will want you in their lives, accept you for who you are, and support and stand beside you when you need them the most. Margie and Donna were always there for my children and me. It is true: *family is more than blood.*

This chapter thus takes me back to the year of 2009, which began with an agonizing event that shattered me to the core. I had never imagined such pain.

22

THE YEAR OF A MIRACLE

My boys and I had a chance to celebrate the 2009 New Year with my family and friends in Georgia. It was two days before our return flight back to California when my mother surprised me and offered to keep Luka, then four years old, with her and my dad for a few months. Then she said she would bring him with her when she would come to visit us in California at the beginning of June. Luka had so much fun in Georgia. He loved being with my parents, my family members, and friends. But most of all, he was getting so much love and attention from everyone there and he was an extremely happy little boy. So, I knew that he would be OK for a few months without me.

Parenting is a continual ride, with overwhelming worries and concerns. My mom was concerned about my health; I was suffering from anemia, and so I was exhausted and looked drained every day. However, by offering her assistance with Luka, she assumed it would have given me some time to take care of myself and get stronger. Luka was turning five and he needed so much energy and attention from me like all five-year-old boys require from their parents, and the worst part was that he was a very fussy and picky eater like me, but he was truly worse than me. Luka's palate was so sensitive that he simply didn't like the texture or taste of almost everything. He would refuse to eat and cry every time I tried to feed him. I was frustrated and had a hard time figuring out what to cook so that he would get the right amount of nutrients on a daily basis. His favorite food was just plain bread and pizza, and it still is! Although today he still doesn't like certain things, overall he will eat nearly every fruit and vegetable as well as everything else I provide. Surprisingly, Luka would eat better with my mom and dad if I wasn't present. He wouldn't dare complain to my mom about food like he did with me. When I was a child, my mother had always been very tough with me when it came to eating. She never raised her voice, yet just one stern look from her was more than enough for me to finish whatever she put on my plate. Honestly, she didn't need to be strict with Luka; just her presence was sufficient. For that reason, I didn't worry even the tiniest bit about leaving my son with my parents.

Chiko's and my relationship was different. We grew up together and he looked more like my little brother than my son. We chatted a lot at night before going to bed, shared stories, and laughed loudly. Chiko invariably was a huge help for me at home. After coming home from work, there were days when I couldn't do anything because I was worn out and without even asking, he would willingly do dishes, clean up, and help me feed Luka. He was unusually caring, insightful, and a very protective son and older brother. He also loved tasting new things and was a good eater. Chiko was the man in the house, and at the same time he was a wonderful teenager and the joy of my life.

January 7, 2009, the day after Chiko's and my return to California, we were on the way to school that morning when Chiko suddenly started throwing up and afterwards collapsed in the car. Everything materialized so fast that the only thing I remember thinking was that he must have gotten food poisoning from something that he ate on the plane. Shortly after, we ended up in the emergency room at John Muir Health, Walnut Creek Medical Center. Donna showed up right away in the hospital after my call and we were both sitting in the lobby when the emergency department case manager approached us and told me that she would take me inside to see my son. But she warned me that he would not look the way I expected him to. I didn't pay attention to what she said, I just automatically followed her. I was desperate to see my boy. As I'm typing these words I can hear my heart beat, feel its pounding in my chest, and my hands are shaking. It is very difficult for me to retrieve the image I saw in the room where my fourteen-year-old son was being attended to. When I entered the room, my frightened eyes caught sight of Chiko. He was placed on a table with a tube inserted down his throat. He was in a coma and was breathing with the assistance of ventilator and IVs were taped on the inside of his elbow. He was surrounded by doctors and nurses. I quickly reached him, grabbed his hand, and looked at him in dismay. I didn't believe what I was witnessing in that room was real. Everyone looked intense. With my panicky voice, I kept repeating, "What happened to my son? What happened to my Chiko?" The doctor was standing on the opposite side of the table, facing me. He looked at me and with an earnest voice, he said that Chiko experienced a ruptured brain aneurysm, which caused bleeding into the brain (hemorrhagic stroke) and it was life threatening. I was staring at the doctor in confusion and had no clue what he was talking about. I didn't know what a brain aneurysm was and had never heard of it. In my mind, I was getting furious and thinking about my son, who never had any health issues and had always been one hundred percent healthy; despite that, he was in critical condition. In a few seconds, I burst out crying so loudly that I couldn't control my emotions. I became hysterical, blaming doctors and everyone in that room that they were killing my son. I kept screaming, "My child is healthy. He doesn't have any health issues. He can't have a brain aneurysm, it's impossible." Donna was standing next to me, she was trying to calm me down, but no one could stop me at that moment; I lost control. The emergency doctor tried to explain to me what a brain aneurysm was. "It is a weak, bulging spot on the side of a brain artery, like a thin balloon and when it ruptures, it causes the blood to be released into the head and it becomes life threatening," he said. But then he added that Chiko was lucky that he was a very healthy kid. I responded to him with my anguished crying voice, "My son is lucky, because he is healthy, yet his life is still in danger. That's all you can say?" I wanted to hear from a doctor that my son was going to be fine and there was nothing to worry about. But I was irrational and fully lost. I plummeted into the depth of hopelessness and in that very moment I was desperate to be awakened from that horrifying dream. With so much sobbing and wailing, I got lightheaded, lost balance, and fell in the hallway, outside Chiko's room. I remember the nurses helped to get me into a wheelchair. I was a wreck and thrashed in pain, and negative thoughts hijacked my mind. I was pondering over Chiko's father, Erekle, and I thought he wanted to take my son away from me. *First it was Erekle, then Giorgi, and now Chiko?* I asked that question and then immediately I answered to myself, *No, I'm not going to let that happen. My son has a long life ahead of him. He's got so much to learn and do. He loves life and he is a good kid!* Tears kept rolling down my cheeks. As I was sitting in the wheelchair, I spontaneously took a sandwich with roast beef and spinach out from my handbag and devoured it. I realized that it wasn't time for me to be anemic or weak. I had to get stronger to be there for my son; Chiko needed me. While the nurses were intensively observing Chiko, they also kept their eyes on me. Everyone, including Donna, thought that I would throw up after consuming the whole sandwich. A nurse even gave me a medical sterile plastic tray. They all were concerned about my actions. Shortly after, the emergency doctor entered the room and informed me that they were going to perform endovascular coiling to block the blood flow into the aneurysm and that was the best option for Chiko at that time. He also warned me that it was a dangerous procedure and there was a risk for complications involving the brain.

Once Chiko was taken to the operating room, Donna and I moved to a waiting room. I was anxious, my heart was sinking. Those hours were unbearable. During the waiting time, I went to the bathroom; no one was inside and this is what I recall happened. When I finished washing my hands, I looked at myself in the mirror and instead of seeing a nerve-racked or overwrought face, surprisingly my own reflection through the mirror looked at me in a calm and amiable manner. I became so present that I started fixing my hair, checking my dress, and even got my lipstick out of my handbag and put it on. Then my reflection in the mirror smiled at me as if everything was just the way it should be. That moment seemed to soothe me and somehow affirmed that Chiko was going to be fine. I listened to my heart and found inner peace. I can't tell you whether I accepted or surrendered to the situation at that time, but I definitely let go of fear and anger and trusted how I felt in that instant. In that fleeting moment, I felt good and confident and believed with all my heart that a team of angels in their white coats and scrubs would save my son's life.

In fact, I remember as soon as I left the bathroom, the first thought that came into my mind was, *Your son is in a critical condition and you had time to put lipstick on.* That was my sarcastic *ego* talking to me. I was heading to a waiting room when at the end of the hallway, I glimpsed Chiko's doctor walking towards me. My heart was pounding out of my chest. From the distance, I sensed that the doctor seemed tranquil and as he approached me with his relieved face, he said that the procedure went successfully and Chiko was stable. I quickly embraced him and felt deep, overwhelming gratitude for him and other medical professionals. I felt that January seventh was the day of my son's rebirth with the help of those outstanding doctors and nurses who miraculously saved my boy's life.

The next morning the John Muir emergency nurse came into Chiko's room, where he was in a coma. I was sitting next to his bed and with a warm, damp washcloth I was gently cleaning his hands and chubby fingers. The nurse came up to me and in her tender voice, she said that watching me the day before in the emergency room made her deeply emotional. She cried and when she went home after work, she hugged her fourteen-year-old son and told him that she loved him so much. She said her son asked if she was OK and she replied that she just wanted to make sure that he knew how much she loved him and how grateful and blessed she was that he was in good health. Her eyes were full of tears. She said that we don't appreciate how lucky we are when our children are well, how precious their lives are, and how important it is to give them more love and warmth and attention while they are growing up. We take things for granted until we see firsthand and face something so devastating and painful. She told me that Chiko was a strong boy and believed that he would get through this horrifying experience. Her heartfelt words touched me that day and stayed with me forever. I don't remember her name, but I'd love to take the opportunity through this book to thank her, wherever she is, for everything and just for *being* there for Chiko and me.

Two days after his surgery at John Muir, Chiko was transferred to the Pediatric Intensive Care Unit at Kaiser

Permanente Medical Center in Oakland, where he remained hospitalized for five weeks. After the endovascular coiling, he was kept in an induced coma for two weeks. Those days and weeks were endless, exhausting, and terrifying but at the same time, I recognized how fortunate I was that my son was surrounded by a team of physicians, nurses, respiratory therapists, physical therapists, dietitians, and other specialists who tirelessly worked together every day to keep him alive.

During that traumatic time in the PICU, Chiko also had undergone another surgery, called a surgical clipping, where an incision was made at the back of his neck to expose where the aneurysm was located on his brain. Then a small clip was placed across the base of the aneurysm to block the blood flow into it. When Chiko was finally discharged from the hospital and I brought my son home, I didn't take lightly what a gift I had been given and how incredibly blessed we both were. Two months after being released from the hospital, Chiko miraculously recovered and regained his health. It's been almost twelve years since then and even though I expressed my heartfelt appreciation towards all of those amazing medical professionals at that time, I still don't think it is ever enough to thank doctors and nurses for their patience, devotion, skill, and tireless service. Especially now as I am writing this book in the year of 2020, while so many people lost their loved ones to the COVID-19 pandemic, many lives were saved by our courageous health care professionals. I felt the need to thank all of our world's heroes that are wearing scrubs and other uniforms who put their own health at risk to help those most vulnerable across the world. Thank you all for giving yourself openly with compassion to care for strangers that you might never see again, but you touch the heart of each and every patient along with their families and friends. I think of you all with profound gratitude and awe.

I believe that in every adversity hope is still possible— hope that contains the three most essential ingredients, which we all have within: *light, music,* and *love.* The only thing we need to do is to find and use them. One of my own poems exemplifies my understanding of "hope":

> *When darkness falls around you*
> *See the LIGHT with your closed eyes.*
> *Hear the MUSIC with your ears shut*
> *And feel the LOVE within your heart.*

23

YOUR CHILDREN ARE NOT
YOUR CHILDREN
—KAHLIL GIBRAN

In 2014, Chiko moved to another state where he got a job and began a new life on his own. In fact, when he decided to move out, I was very supportive of his decision and encouraged him to keep his faith and to stay brave no matter how many times he might fail. I told him that without courage, he couldn't find the purpose in his life. I wanted him to find his own strengths to spread his wings and fly. Like a beautiful butterfly, when it emerges from its chrysalis, it struggles to fit through the small opening. If we try to help it by making the hole of the chrysalis bigger, we can permanently harm it with our attempted effort to assist it. Pushing its way out of the chrysalis is what strengthens the butterfly's wings so that it can fly.[30] Hence, I let Chiko fly out of my sight, urged him to follow his own path and push his own way out of struggles that he would encounter. Although I knew the road ahead of him wasn't going to be smooth, I had faith in his own abilities and believed that stepping out of his comfort zone and entering bravely into his own life was the only way he could find out who he really was. Kahlil Gibran narrated in his best-known work, *The Prophet*, the following:

> *Your children are not your children.*
> *They are the sons and daughters of Life's longing for itself.*
> *They come through you but not from you,*
> *And though they are with you, yet they belong not to you.*
> *YOU may give them your love but not your thoughts,*
> *For they have their own thoughts.*
> *You may house their bodies but not their souls,*
> *For their souls dwell in the house of tomorrow,*
> *which you cannot visit, not even in your dreams.*

24

LONGING FOR A CHANGE

Since I moved to California, my main focus was my children and work. I wanted to make sure that I was always there for my kids and also performed my job well. As I was in the media industry for a few years back in Georgia, I had been constantly trying to find a job in the media field in Northern California. At the same time, I was eager to broaden my skills in the arts and entertainment industry by taking intense coursework and training in acting, producing, and voice-over. In addition to that, I was working intensively with my dialect coaches to improve my American accent, which would help me to get more professional opportunities in the arts and media fields. After almost nine and a half years of living and working in Northern California, in 2015, I was called for a change and was brave enough to answer the call without delay. So, I started planning to embark on a new life adventure by moving to Los Angeles, where I could pursue my passion. As I kept encouraging Chiko to stay brave and move forward, in spite of obstacles and failures in his life, I tried to do the same for myself. I was driven by curiosity and was ready to face more challenges in life. Since Chiko was no longer living with us and Luka was in middle school and becoming more independent, I thought that I had some time to ardently focus on the work to which I was so committed. In fact, Donna was my biggest supporter; she believed in my decision and motivated me to move to Southern California with Luka. Although she said she would miss us terribly, she wanted me to follow my heart's desire and not to feel guilty about leaving her.

Prior to my move, my central focus was my children and work. I was socializing on a very limited basis and had dated a couple of times very briefly. Frankly, I only went out on a few dates because my mom pushed me a little bit. She used to tell me that I was a young and beautiful woman and, besides my children and work, I needed to have a social life too; so, I should go out, have some fun, and take a chance on another man. Whenever my mom brought up the topic about men, my response to her was always, "Mom, you know that every time I start dating someone, I either get hurt or disappointed, so I don't want to talk about men." I lived in the fear of being hurt again, being taken advantage of, or not being appreciated and so forth. All of my negative thoughts still stemmed from the past. In truth, the beliefs that I had about men in those days caused me to attract that exact type of person and so, when I dated someone, I was invariably disappointed because of my *own harmful thoughts*. Today, what I accept as truth is that I wasn't failed by those men whom I dated but by my fearful and limited thoughts.

In 2013, I came across Abraham-Hicks' online teachings about *The Law of Attraction*. Abraham-Hicks says, "What you think about activates a vibration within you. What you are living is the evidence of what you are thinking and feeling—every single time."[31] It resonated with me and it made me realize that I was attracting exactly what my thoughts were about men. I actually understood how powerful my thoughts were and I immediately decided to change my beliefs about men, because deep inside, my heart genuinely wanted to meet a healthy, honest, kind, and caring man. Thus, I started focusing on the qualities and characteristics I was looking for in a potential partner.

Even though I didn't know a single soul in Los Angeles, once I moved to the City of Angeles in August 2015, I felt that I was home and not in a strange or unfamiliar place. I felt that I was in the city where not only the weather was fabulous and the sun was smiling down on everyone, but there was a greater sense of possibility to find what I was looking for; I felt that I could evolve without limits there. But on the other hand, it certainly wasn't an easy endeavor to begin my journey with my son alone in LA. Although I had the courage to discover my hidden capabilities, I didn't know what was buried within me then. However, I prayed every day, and this is what I asked: "God, please help me to find my own unique talent and gift that I have within me and to use it wisely. Please guide me. Thank you!"

The first year in Los Angeles was a year of doing an extensive amount of research to enhance my knowledge in the arts and entertainment industry. I carried on sharpening my voice-over and acting skills through workshops, classes, and various training programs where I met friendly, supportive, and talented people. Simultaneously, I was taking every job opportunity that I was offered, whether it was for extras, background jobs, or side gigs. But above all, I was there for Luka to make this transition easy and smooth for him; he was still terribly missing his old home, school, and his best friend, Sebastian, although they FaceTimed each other every day. Most of all, he missed Donna and Hanley and their presence in his life. It took more than a year before Luka fully acclimated to his new life in Southern California.

25

LOS ANGELES, CALIFORNIA (2016-2017)

At the beginning of 2016, I met my friend Anna through one of the acting schools that we both attended in Los Angeles. We instantly became good friends. Anna is married with two beautiful children—a girl and a boy. She and her family are Armenian, originally from the Middle East. Anna is exceptionally generous, kind, caring, and smart, and one of the sweetest young women I've ever met. In 2017, Anna and I were quite committed to making our own web series and publishing it online in order to get our voices and faces out there. In the middle of February, we shot our first episode at my place and after we cleaned everything up, Anna asked me to go out and celebrate our new venture together. I was feeling a little bit under the weather that evening and really didn't want to go anywhere, but she insisted, so I couldn't turn her down.

We ended up having a lovely dinner in one of the restaurants in the city and I was very delighted that I went out with her. The music and atmosphere in the restaurant were so serene and relaxing. I took my phone out from my purse and asked Anna to take a selfie of us. Two men were having dinner at the table next to us. One man, perhaps in his late seventies or early eighties, was wearing a very stylish hat and looked very classy. The other one was an attractive middle-aged man, possibly in his early fifties. He was fit and well dressed, with dark hair. The younger man offered to take a picture of me and Anna. Without hesitation, I passed my phone to him and, with pleasure, he took a few photos of us. Then he asked if they could join us for the night. At first, we both were reluctant to say anything, but ultimately, I spoke up and said, "Yes, of course."

They introduced themselves and revealed that they were stepfather and son. (In order to protect their privacy, they will be referred to by the same names as they were called in my first book, *A Hummingbird's Nest*.) The stepfather, Carlos, sat next to Anna, and the son, Marco, sat very close to me on the sofa. I felt a little uncomfortable and moved myself away from him a little bit. Marco instantly became very curious about me. He asked about my originality, how long I had been in the US, what I did, and so forth. I briefly told him about myself, that I had two sons and I moved to Los Angeles from Northern California with my younger son, Luka, a couple of years ago.

Without even asking, Marco just started talking about himself briefly; he lived and had his office in Beverly Hills. And then, out of the blue, Carlos asked me to dance with him. There was a singer with a live band in the restaurant, and they were playing Latin American music. I promptly got up and joined Carlos on the dance floor. Carlos was an amazing dancer and while I danced with him, Marco told Anna that he would really, really like to see me again. Anna knew that Marco was very interested in me. After I finished dancing with Carlos, I went back and sat next to Marco. He immediately wanted to hug me but I automatically pushed him back and said, "No hugging." He apologized and very kindly told me that he would love to see me again, then politely asked for my cell phone number. To be honest with you, Marco seemed like a very nice man, yet something within me made me unsure about seeing him again. I liked Carlos though. Anyway, I gave him my number and we all said goodbye to one another. After we left the restaurant, Anna told me that she really liked Marco and that if he called me, she said, "Please, please, give him a chance. He seems like a good, decent man."

26

THE FIRST DATE

I was shooting one of our series' episodes with Anna in the middle of March 2017 when I received a call from Marco. It had been almost a month since we met at the restaurant in the city and I was really surprised to hear from him. He told me that he was in the hospital because his stepfather, Carlos, had been very sick and they had been going back and forth to the emergency room for the past week. He said while he was in the hospital, watching his dad so ill and weak, he was thinking about the last time that he danced. He recalled that the last time his stepfather danced was the day when we first met in that restaurant. He said thinking about that made him want to see me, so he called me right away from the hospital and asked when I was available to have dinner with him. That's how our journey began.

On our first date, Marco and I exchanged our stories and told each other about our pasts. He told me about his previous relationships. He was thirty-one when he met his soon-to-be wife and fell in love with her so quickly that he proposed to her in six weeks and they got married six months later. The only problem he had was that she wanted to have kids and he didn't. Because of that, eight years later, they decided to divorce. Subsequently, he had two fiancés, but he never married either of them for the same reason. He said he hated kids then and never wanted them, probably because he had a lousy childhood. But when he got a little bit older, he regretted that he didn't have any children. And he was actually glad that I had two sons.

Marco was born in the Los Angeles area and was just six months old when his father left him and his mom. Marco's mother was very young and raised him by herself. But she was very mean and harsh on Marco, always screaming and throwing things at him. Sometimes she'd say that she wanted to kill him, and as a little boy, Marco repeated the same things, throwing things back at her and yelling at her, saying that he wanted to kill her too. He was six years old when his mom met Carlos and they got married when Marco was eight. Carlos had a horrible temper then, and he was always yelling at Marco's mom. They used to fight every day and Marco hated being with them, especially going out with them together, because of that. Even though he had a younger sister, he couldn't wait to grow up and leave his parents' house. So basically, Marco's childhood was miserable and he never had any peace or love. When he turned eighteen, he left his parents' house and never went back. He took care of himself, started working and building his own life. He never got any financial help from his family but he became independent at a very young age. Sales and marketing really interested him, so he focused on moving in that professional direction. Finally, years and years later, he established his own real estate business, worked extremely hard, and created a secure life for himself. He also considered himself very lucky. Additionally, years later, he became closer to his step-dad, and since then they had a more peaceful relationship.

After our first date, I don't know why, but I felt a strong connection and some sort of familiarity with Marco. I was certain that I wanted to see him again; he treated me very respectfully, elegantly and in a caring manner. When I shared this news with Luka, he was thrilled to hear that I was finally going out with someone. He even revealed his secret and told me that it was one of his Christmas wishes for me to have a boyfriend. He indeed wanted a man, not only for me, but in his life, too.

27

MARCO AND US

When Marco and I started dating, everything was unfolding on our path so easily that I never thought or believed, after all of these years, I could meet someone so special. We had a lot in common and gave importance to similar things in life, as well as deriving pleasure from similar things. We both loved poetry and Marco, like me, used to write poems when he was a little child. He loved when I recited poems to him. We enjoyed playing piano together and I used to teach him pieces that I learned from my mom in my youth. We would often go out to dance and could dance endlessly as we had similar tastes in music. We were attracted to each other not only physically but emotionally. Marco was very tender and gentle towards me and I was strongly drawn to him by some unexplainable force. My heart fully opened up to him. Furthermore, we were both driven and hardworking individuals, but what I mainly admired about Marco was that he was an attentive listener. He would sit and listen to me for hours and I would talk and, in a zestful manner, share with him all of the things that I felt were blessings in my own life. Marco used to call me a "hummingbird" because he said I was physically little, very curious, sweet, and always moving. Sometimes, he thought I was nervous or afraid of something as I was flitting around a room. I loved my new name as much as I love hummingbirds. When Marco and I were together, time seemed irrelevant; we were deeply engaged, laughed a lot, and sweetly enjoyed our moments. Sometimes, I even felt that I had known him for my entire life.

First and foremost, Marco's presence in Luka's life was creating many significant moments and memories. They used to get along well with each other and they talked a lot about everything: school, sports, especially basketball and LeBron James. LeBron wasn't only Luka's most favorite player but he was Marco's, too. They played games, joked, and had fun together. Luka tremendously enjoyed it when Marco was at our place. He felt more confident as a young man when Marco was around. Luka had always been a very picky eater, and at age thirteen, there were still a few things (one of them was eggs) that he wouldn't eat, no matter what. One morning, Marco, Luka, and I were having breakfast and Marco asked Luka to try a little bit of an omelet to see if he liked the taste of it. I was sure that Luka was going to say a big *no* with a grimace but surprisingly, he picked a little piece and ate it. I couldn't believe that Luka was actually eating eggs! That's how much respect and trust he had towards Marco. He was so happy having Marco in his life that he didn't want to disappoint him under any circumstance.

28

At the end of May 2017, Luka's school was over and I drove him up to Northern California to spend the summer with Donna, Hanley, and his friends. He missed living up there and he was anxiously looking forward to that trip the entire year. Luka has always loved being with Donna since he was a little boy. They played board games, watched movies, and their favorite cooking shows on TV. He also did lots of house chores and helped Donna in the garden. But what Luka loved the most at Donna's, besides his pal, Hanley, was the special treats that she made for him. She would bake Luka's favorite chocolate chip cookies and brownies. Leaving Luka with Donna for the summer gave me more time to focus on the web series that I was producing with Anna and on the other work, as well. Needless to say, I was also very happy to be able to spend more time with Marco to get to know him better.

Marco traveled periodically for his business. He was managing and running his own real estate investment firm and with his devotion, talent, and persistence, he was very successful in his work. He had a strong desire to work hard, expand, and make more money. He lived a luxurious life. I respected his diligence and hard work and he appreciated and respected mine. We, therefore allowed each other to have our own space and freedom to pursue our own individual goals and aspirations and we valued the time we spent together.

Marco loved taking me out to the most exclusive and expensive restaurants in the LA area, but he always said that no one could make soups as delicious as mine. I believed he was telling the truth since every time I made any type of soup dish, he would eat not only one portion of it, but two or three. That meant so much to me because neither of my exes nor my own children ever appreciated my cooking as much as Marco did. Honestly, I am definitely not as good of a cook as my mom, Donna, Enro, or my grandmothers were. Unlike them, I was always a picky eater, so cooking was never really my passion. However, regardless of my fussy eating, I always cooked healthy meals for my children because that's how I was raised. But I wholeheartedly enjoyed cooking various dishes every time Marco came to see me during the summer. I was in love and wanted to express this powerful feeling through every little thing I could do for him.

⤡

After Marco and I had become physically intimate, my lifestyle dramatically changed. Every time we were together, I either ended up in urgent care or the ER. It started like this:

The first week in June 2017, I rushed to the urgent care center because I was experiencing severe pain when I went to the bathroom; I could hardly pee. After an examination and getting my lab results back, I was diagnosed with a bladder infection and a vaginal yeast infection. I had never had a bladder infection before; it was very painful. However, the urgent care doctor told me that in a new relationship, this kind of thing could happen, especially if I had not had a partner for a long time. I had to get used to his "flora." I was relieved that I had nothing serious. But once I got better, I ended up in urgent care again with a vaginal infection that was most likely caused by the antibiotics I was taking for my bladder infection. That's what my physician told me. By June 20, 2017, I had already visited the urgent care department six or seven times for the same type of infections. In the early morning on this same day, I was desperate to get to the hospital but was so sick that I was having a hard time driving my car. I called my friend, Doris, whom I had also met at one of the acting schools in LA. Doris is a very talented artist who is vibrant, determined, caring, smart, and hardworking with a strong personality. She is married and has a lovely stepdaughter. When I called her, she was on her way to an acting class. I told her that I woke up that morning and felt like I was going to explode. I couldn't pee at all and in the last couple of days, I had a difficult time going to the bathroom even if I pushed really hard. Doris was mad that I was driving by myself in this condition and didn't call anyone for help. She said right away that she would see me at the hospital and that she was very concerned about my condition.

I don't know how I parked my car or got into the emergency room. I could hardly stand on my own and as soon as I entered the ER, I fell on the floor and started screaming, "Help . . . help me . . . Please help me!" Nurses quickly rushed to me and took me directly to an exam room. The only thing I said was that I couldn't pee and was in agony. I was gasping and thought that I was dying and was screaming in pain when the nurses got me to lie down on the exam table. They speedily proceeded to catheterize me to relieve the pressure on my bladder. After a while, I finally left the exam room and came out, where Doris was waiting for me. I looked devastated, frightened, and weary. I told Doris that I had a catheter in me and I burst into tears. Doris looked at me appalled. She was at a loss for words. She put her hand on my shoulder, hugged me, and tried to comfort me. She couldn't believe that I needed a catheter and she asked why all of these things were happening to me. She assumed that Marco perhaps had some type of medical condition and that he needed to get checked. In fact, I spoke with an ER doctor about Marco but she said that it had nothing to do with him. Because I had both a bladder infection and an yeast infection, and took so many antibiotics and other medications, that probably could have been the reason why I couldn't pee. My system completely shut down. They did a blood test and other lab tests and informed me that I was healthy otherwise. Doris was still unable to digest all of this. She was driving me home in dismay and said, "I still don't get it. You're a healthy young woman, but you need a catheter. Why? Because you had sex with your boyfriend? And because you had a few infections? I've never heard of anything like this in my entire life. A woman having sex with a partner and needing a catheter because she can't pee? What did you guys do? For me, it feels like you have an allergic reaction to Marco. This sounds unbelievable . . ." Doris was angry, but at the same time, she laughed in disbelief. Although I was traumatized and woeful, I started laughing and crying at the same time. I thought that all of this was bizarre. I had never had any health issues or any of these types of problems with my previous relationships. Maybe once in my life I had a mild yeast infection and that was it. The doctor told me that it would take some time for me to get used to being with Marco. In the meantime, I had to take care of myself.

When Doris brought me home, she asked if I was going to call Marco and tell him about what happened. She said that he was part of this, and he should be with me to help me through this. I told her that he was leaving town for a business trip on that same day, for just a few days and I didn't want to stress him out about my issues. Honestly, I didn't really want him to see me wearing a catheter bag under my clothes. It was so embarrassing; I felt awful. I was so emotional—in tears. I would never have imagined that I would need a catheter to pee just because I was sleeping with my boyfriend. As Doris tried consoling me, she also encouraged me to call and tell Marco about this event sooner rather than later. She said, "Marco needs to be here next to you to comfort you and give you his love and attention and take care of you. This wouldn't have happened to you if he wasn't in your life. If he considers himself your boyfriend and loves you—and I'm sure he does—then he should be concerned about your condition and be here with you. So, please don't feel uncomfortable or embarrassed about it. People get sick; we're all human beings. I would suggest that you do some meditation every day. It'll help you heal and recover faster. You're a strong and healthy woman and you'll be just fine." I don't know what I would have done in those days, in Los Angeles, without my two beautiful soul mates, Doris and Anna. They both were there for me and supported me throughout this ordeal. Their love and care and friendship were priceless and they will forever have a special place in my heart.

After Doris left, I called Marco and told him everything. He was already out of town for his business meeting. He couldn't believe that this was happening to me and thought that the whole thing was surreal. He said that when he got back, he was willing to go with me to see a doctor, even though what was happening to me wasn't really his fault. Then he asked if I needed anything. I replied that I had everything and I was OK. I wasn't OK though; I lied. I was scared, anxious, and depressed. But I didn't want to reveal how I felt. I didn't want to bother him with my ongoing infections and my stress about being catheterized. I was mortified. Although I was overwhelmed by everything that was happening, I didn't want to sound like a despondent and needy person lest it would push him away from me. My ego kept reminding me of how *independent, strong,* and *positive* I was, that I could take care of myself, and that I didn't need to be rescued by my boyfriend. That night I couldn't sleep. I kept tossing and turning all night and was unable to find a comfortable position in bed. I got up slowly, feeling horrible, went to the bathroom, undressed, and took a shower. I was standing under the shower head, staring at the bag hanging on my naked body. The catheter was so bothersome that I was irritated and desperate to take it off and throw it away. After I came out of the bathroom, I tried to meditate but instead I cried all night long.

Marco was supposed to be away only for a couple of days. He never called me the next day or the day after. I didn't call him either—my *ego* prevented me from doing so. He was gone much longer than I had expected (later on I found out that after his business trip, he flew to Hawaii to have a few days of vacation for himself). I gave him space and waited for him to call me. In the meantime, I was hurt and disappointed in not hearing from him while he was away. Now, as opposed to calling Marco and telling him the truth about how I felt and that I needed him to be with me at that very difficult time, I chose to *lie*, first to myself and then to him. Why? Because of my *fearful thoughts* of losing him if I bothered him too much. It's fear that limited me. It's fear that disempowered me. It's fear that held me back. It's fear that gave me nightmares. I wasn't yet ready to face, acknowledge, and challenge that fear. I reckoned that Marco was a very busy man with an extraordinary amount of obligations at his firm and if I burdened him with my problems in my fragile emotional state, he could have withdrawn from me. Obviously, I was in love and didn't want that to happen so I stayed untruthful to myself and towards him as well. Now, was it Marco's fault that I was home by myself, miserable, and sad? Definitely not!

If I wanted to have Marco next to me, I could have easily called and asked him to come and stay with me after he was done with his business trip. And if he had some excuse that he needed to go somewhere else and didn't have time for me then, at least, I would have learned sooner than later that he really didn't care about me and wasn't serious about this relationship. But what did I do? I waited and waited, with the *hope* that he would call. *Was he supposed to read my mind?* He must have assumed because I didn't call him during his time away that I was OK and didn't want to be bothered.

Donna was calling me every day, checking on me as to how I was feeling and handling everything. I was so lucky that, at that time, Luka was having an awesome summer with Donna and his friends. Thankfully, he wasn't seeing my wretchedly uncomfortable face and gloomy persona on a daily basis. In addition to all of the roles that Donna has played in my life (like being my mentor, mother, friend, and my children's guardian), in those trying days she had also become my therapist. I couldn't ask for a better therapist than her; we often spoke on the phone for hours. She listened to my emotional, crying voice patiently and tried to uplift my spirit and made me laugh. I laughed and cried with her a lot. I shared more with Donna than with my mom at that time, since I didn't want to worry my mom about all of the things that I was going through. I could feel that Donna was upset that Marco wasn't there with me from the very beginning when I first got my catheter and was so dejected, bewildered, and tearful. But she didn't say anything to avoid hurting my feelings, because she knew how much I cared about him.

One week later, I was in the hospital, the nurse removed my catheter and told me to go to the bathroom. So, I went to the hospital bathroom, trying to pee; my bladder was filled up, but I couldn't do it. I got my cell phone out of my handbag and called Donna. She was in her kitchen I could hear that she was chopping something. I was crying and told her that I was trying so hard but couldn't pee. Donna right away said, "Don't worry, honey, start breathing." We both began inhaling and exhaling so deep that she felt like she had to go to the bathroom, but I was still unable to do so. Then she said that I should turn the water on in the sink, and let it run. Sometimes the sound of running water helps. I turned the water on and started moving around the bathroom vigorously, doing everything I could, but had no success. I was broken and distraught. That was the most terrifying feeling: I wanted to pee so badly, but I couldn't. I was sobbing like a little girl while pacing back and forth. Donna was still on the phone and was trying to calm me down. She said that I was too stressed and that was one of the reasons I couldn't go. I decided to go out and walk in the hallway a little bit, hoping that it would help. I even went to the cafeteria and got a big cup of hot tea, some ice water, and cold juice. Nothing helped me. Shortly after, Marco picked me up from the hospital and took me home with my catheter. I never asked him anything about his trip. I was so happy to see him that I merely wanted to focus on us and on the things that we enjoyed doing together. At home, I put on *The Blue Danube*, a waltz by Strauss and showed Marco how to waltz. We practiced dancing slowly the entire evening. He was so passionate about dancing with me that he didn't want to stop. He told me that he had never danced a waltz before because didn't know how to; now he loved it so much that he wanted to dance with me all night.

∾

It was the Fourth of July. I was home by myself, sitting on the couch and reading the script for a big audition I had coming up the next day. The role was for an Eastern European dance instructor, in a feature film, and I was repetitively reading my lines aloud. But prior to the audition, I had a very important appointment early that morning. I was getting my catheter removed. It had already been two weeks since I had the catheter inserted and I couldn't wait for the moment to finally be free of it. And most importantly, I didn't want to show up at my audition with a catheter. It would've been a disaster playing a dance teacher with a bag hanging under my dress. Anyway, I was still ready for my audition whether it was with or without a catheter.

Marco wanted to take me to the beach club to celebrate the Fourth of July with his friends but he also understood that I couldn't go in this condition. So, he went by himself and I was really OK with that. I wanted him to go and have fun with his friends. I didn't have a problem with him going without me. But what really hurt me was when he called around 6:00 p.m. and asked if I still had any meatball soup leftover from the day before. I replied that I didn't because one of my good friends, who was helping Anna and me with camera work for our web series and who had not seen me in a while, had just come by to visit and I offered him some soup and other things I had at home for lunch. Marco said sarcastically, "Oh, I understand! You offer other men soup too? How many men come to your house to eat your soup? But that's fine. I wanted to come and see you, but if you don't have any soup then I'll go home instead and have some of those cheese breads you gave me the other day." I was really annoyed by his comment about the soup and other men. I made it clear to him and said, "When I have guests, I always offer them my hospitality and kindness, including food, especially if they're my good friends. That's how I was raised. That's what my parents and grandparents and great-grandparents used to do." Then I asked him, if he really wanted to see me that day or if he just wanted to come to have soup. "Both," he replied. I was very upset and told him that I had to go. I had no desire to continue that conversation with him.

He tried to reach me several times to apologize by calling and texting. He texted, "Objectively, life is shorter for me than you. What is left for me to do is to live lightly, laugh, love, be kind, and have fun. If any one of these ingredients is missing, the recipe is incomplete, and the taste of life sours. My humor is not meant to offend you. However, I see that it does. It's a shame, and I apologize."

I replied, "Unfortunately, my understanding of your humor is lacking in precision. I don't do well with innuendo or veiled humor. To make the recipe complete for us, we need to have concise communication in all aspects of life. I love to laugh as long as I understand the joke, but I didn't feel that way after our conversation. Thanks for your apology."

He texted back, "Dear Russo, you understood my reference, and it annoyed you. The joke about men coming to eat your soup was just that. I was planning to come see you without the soup, of course. However, I couldn't reach you. Moving forward, I wish you a positive outcome with the doctor tomorrow. Good night." I was so sad. The tears from my eyes kept on falling while sitting on the couch, holding the script, and reading my lines.

Now by looking back at that day, I was exasperated by the catheter and was already uncomfortable when Marco called. Then his comments about men and soup added another uncomfortable layer upon the existing one and it irritated me even more. So, instead of writing those formal and dignified texts to each other, I could have simply asked him to pick up dinner for both of us and come to my place because I missed him and wanted to be with him. But I chose not to, since my *ego* was hurt. It wasn't Marco's fault that I was sitting on the couch alone and crying! Was it? Or perhaps it was something else. Now, I know what it was. I wasn't feeling well and wanted him to pick up dinner for both of us and come to my place and show how much he cared about me. I wanted him to do all of that on his own, without me asking or telling him. I always believed that when your partner or loved ones are sick, you don't need an invitation or a reminder to go and see them or pick up some food or medication for them. I considered that they were normal caring gestures.

Today I believe that Marco's behavior kept reminding me of an aspect that I didn't like about *myself*, my inner conflicts that I hadn't resolved. The truth was that I was constantly suppressing this discord. Therefore, there were days in our relationship that I was heartbroken because I didn't say what I really wanted or how I truly felt. *I was hurt not because of his actions, but because of my fears.*

~~~~~~

It was early afternoon, and I was sitting in the casting room waiting to audition, with my catheter hidden beneath a beautiful long dress that I wore to conceal it. I was anxious, breathing deeply, and secretly checking my catheter bag. No one would have noticed it unless the casting director asked me to show him some moves from a typical Georgian folk dance. If that was the case, then I knew that the catheter bag would've dropped for sure, like it happened a week earlier outside a grocery store. I was rushing out of the store and suddenly, the bag almost fell on my foot. I quickly put my grocery bags on the ground, picked up the catheter bag, and reattached it to the strap on my leg. I was *so embarrassed*. What was I thinking? I was crazy to go to the audition with my catheter, knowing that if I booked a job, it would have been absurd of me to be on set and working for hours with a catheter attached. I would have been running back and forth to the bathroom while filming. Plus, the doctor told me that morning that I had to keep my catheter for another two, or possibly three, weeks before they could remove it. I was devastated about the news, but I pretended that everything was just fine and that I could do anything I focused on. I didn't want to acknowledge or accept the fact that I was fitted with a catheter, nor did I want to disappoint my manager who arranged the audition. Instead of telling her that it would be impracticable for me to audition in this condition, I strived to prove to her that I was ready to do anything regardless of the circumstances. Ultimately, I didn't book that job; thank God!

Still, in those days, the word "no" was so hard for me to say. I didn't want to create any unpleasant experience with anyone or let them down. Throughout my journey, whenever I used the word "no" or couldn't do something for others, some people were really disappointed and upset. And that made me feel guilty, since I never wanted to displease anyone. However, what I learned from those experiences is that the reason why *they* were disappointed was that they were used to my accommodation and, therefore, they always had the same expectations from me. Suddenly, breaking that pattern and saying *no* to them didn't sound like me. That's what caused confusion and hurt so I needed to learn how to set boundaries and start respecting myself first. In 2017, I wasn't ready to fully change my habit of pleasing others first and begin saying *yes* to myself; I still struggled to say *no* (due to *fear* of not being liked or accepted by others). But I was getting a little bit better than I was years earlier—or was I?

After the audition that day, I went to a nearby park for a little walk and some fresh air. I felt disheartened and uncomfortable. I decided to sit down underneath a huge sycamore tree and just as I closed my eyes, Marco called. When I answered, he sounded regretful and asked how I was doing. I was both saddened and irritated. I said, "Marco, it's bad enough not being able to pee by myself, but I'm really upset by the way you treated me on the phone yesterday. I thought you would come and see me. It was Fourth of July . . . and the only thing you wanted was my soup!" I was getting very emotional. "Let me tell you this; when you take me out to those fancy restaurants for dinner, it's not that I want to go to those places to eat. Please don't get me wrong. I appreciate going out, and I'm grateful that you want to take me. But you know that I don't eat anything that late in the evening, and I'm not desperate to go to the hottest restaurants in town. For me, the most important thing is that when we go to those places, I just want to be with *you* and spend time with *you*. That's what I want. Because I care about you, and I'm happy with you. The rest is secondary." I reached an emotional peak and was ready to burst into tears but I was trying so hard to hold myself back. My voice was a little shaky. "What you said yesterday showed me that you just wanted to come and see me only if I had *soup* for you. That hurt me . . . How would you feel if you were in my situation? And now you're saying that you wanted to come? If you did, you didn't need my invitation; you would have come. But you didn't, did you?" I suddenly paused. I started feeling very uncomfortable and told Marco that I had to go home. He was at a loss for words, couldn't say anything, and then said, "OK, go, go, and I'll call you later."

As soon as I hung up the phone, I checked the catheter and saw that I was bleeding because the catheter bag's contents were red. I wanted to get up, but I had severe pain in my stomach. I was squirming to ease the pain, yet it increased dramatically, and I couldn't even move. I was so scared and immediately called 911. I survived that day, though I got another infection that was caused by the catheter. I prayed every day and night to be freed from it. At last, after a month of being tethered in this demoralizing condition before I went to the hospital again, I prayed and asked God to help me come home *free* and *happy*.

As I was still not able to go to the bathroom on my own, the nurse at the hospital tried to teach me how to catheterize myself. She told me that I couldn't keep the catheter in any longer and I had to learn self-catheterization. Otherwise, I would get more and more infections, and the doctor didn't want me to get used to relying on a catheter. I was so frustrated and scared that I kept telling the nurse that when she put the catheter in, it was too painful, and I couldn't even imagine putting it in by myself. I repeated over and over, "I can't do this." The nurse was very patient and extremely kind. She explained to me that self-catheterization wasn't as painful as catheterization by someone else. The catheter they used was much larger than the one I was going to use on my own. It was very thin and much easier to insert. She asked me to try it once, and if I couldn't do it, I could talk to my doctor. She also gave me little time to think about it. I was agitated and sitting on the exam table silently and, momentarily, a thought arose in my head: *What happens if you are in an airplane flying over the ocean and there is someone (that someone would need to be a female for sure) who can't pee and requires immediate assistance?* Feeling invigorated, I responded to myself quietly, *I can help only if I learn how to catheterize myself first.* (I know this sounds crazy, but it felt real; it inspired me to learn self-catheterization because I knew firsthand how painful, vexing, and dangerous it could be for anyone not being able to pee.) So, I told the nurse right away that I was ready to do it. And I did it! Honestly, it wasn't that difficult or painful. I got so emotional that I couldn't stop my tears of joy as I was so grateful and relieved. The nurse was happy, too. God bless her—she was really impressed because she hadn't been expecting me to do it so well on my first try, because for the first twenty minutes in the exam room, I only complained how painful that was previously, refused to learn self-catheterization, and looked so frightened.

Finally, when I got home that day, I took a catheter out from my bag and ran straight to the bathroom. But before I opened it to use it, I decided to try to pee by myself. That was one of the most unforgettable moments in my life. I was sitting on the toilet and holding my breath and, suddenly, peed without any difficulty. I started screaming, "I can pee. I can peeeeeeeeeeee . . . Oh my God . . . I can pee! I can't believe this . . . Thank you, God! Thank you, thank you, thank you!" I was screaming so loudly and crying and laughing at the same time that the entire universe could experience that incredible scene of jubilation. I was exhilarated, hugging, and kissing and congratulating myself endlessly. Since then, every time I go to the bathroom and pee, I say "thank you."

This surreal and tumultuous experience taught me something very valuable in this lifetime. I had never appreciated my own body the way I do now. My body is the house of my spirit and I need to nurture, love, and be thankful for it. We only have a very short time on this Earth and we need to protect our body and not take it for granted. Nothing is permanent; everything physical is temporary, and I want to make sure, for the rest of my life, that I stay conscious and aware of it.

The other side of Marco was that he had a very big ego; he liked calling himself a king and wanted to be a winner in everything, particularly when we played games together. He hated to lose. Though I never took it seriously and neither competed nor was determined to win anything, I just enjoyed being with him and focused on the things that I loved about him. Marco was also obsessed about his possessions, especially about his Ferrari. Even though there were some red flags about his behavior I was in love and chose to ignore them. I didn't want to acknowledge that side of Marco and I was in denial. I believed that he was the right person for me and didn't want to think otherwise.

It was a gorgeous, warm morning in August 2017. The sun poured through our car windows and Marco was driving his Ferrari as we were headed to Laguna Beach, California. He was driving so fast that it caused me to spill a little bit of coffee on my clothes. I was holding my coffee cup in one hand (because there was no cup holder in the car) while I tried to take out a chocolate croissant from the bakery bag, but Marco stopped me. If I don't eat something in the morning, I tend to end up with low blood sugar and I can get lightheaded, dizzy, or sometimes even faint. But I didn't tell that to Marco; I didn't want to make a big fuss about it. Once again, I ignored myself completely and tried to be nice to appease him. Would it have been a big fuss to tell him the truth? I don't know what I was thinking! He said that we'd be at the hotel soon so we could eat there. I responded, "Even if I eat the croissant, I won't make a mess, but don't worry, I can wait." I knew he was worried about his car and he kept glancing over at me while I was sipping my coffee. He was so obsessed with that car that he didn't want me to spill anything so I was very careful. Then he asked, "Do you like my car?"

"Actually, I don't," I replied stiffly and quickly, but was that my *honest answer*? Maybe. Or was that response caused by the discomfort I was experiencing in the car? Possibly! Actually, I never felt comfortable in that car though I still appreciated that Marco enjoyed it. I knew how prestigious, classy, luxurious, and valuable a Ferrari was and it was absolutely a great car for *him* because he loved it, but not for *me*. Marco was a little offended with my response. He told me that I had no idea how hard he worked in his life to be able to buy that car. That was his dream. I understood what he was saying and I recognized what a hardworking man he was. But I told him that even if I had enough money to be able to buy that car, I wouldn't because a sports car wasn't my style. I wasn't comfortable in it, but I was glad that he had it. And that was my sincere response. Then with a smile, I told him that I liked big cars and he replied sarcastically, "OK. Hopefully, your next boyfriend will have a truck!" I smiled; I knew he was being silly and I didn't respond. I was starting to get dizzy and asked him to slow down, because I wasn't feeling well. He got scared and quickly reached for the box of protein bars behind his seat and told me to eat the bar and croissant so that I could feel better. Luckily, that prevented me from almost fainting in the car that day. Again, my fearful mind held me back from speaking up.

Once we arrived at the hotel, we checked in and while we were standing in the lobby and admiring the magnificent view of Laguna Beach, Marco wrapped his arms around me and told me that he was so happy to be there with me. I replied that I was happy, too! Then he quickly touched his lips. He had a small blister on his lip; he had told me earlier that, once in a while, he would get this small blister particularly when he was out in the sun, and it only happened maybe once a year or even every two years. But he said it was nothing to worry about and it wasn't contagious. I wasn't concerned about Marco's blister at all. I told him that every now and then I got one or two pimples on my face too. It wasn't a big deal and I didn't understand why he was worried about his little blister—it wasn't even that noticeable. So, I kissed him right away to make him feel comfortable.

We had a few exceptionally blissful and passionate days together. We swam and played in the waves, climbed up some huge rocks, and watched the beautiful ocean waves at sunset. We danced, played games, walked on the beach, talked, kissed, and laughed a lot. The first night at Laguna Beach, I revealed my true feelings to Marco while we were sitting on the hotel patio, where we had an outstanding view of the ocean and the full moon. I gave him a rolled-up piece of paper with a ribbon wrapped around it. He was exuberant and began untying the ribbon. When he unrolled the paper and saw that I had written a poem for him, he read it. But then he wanted to hear the poem in my voice, so he asked me to read it out loud to him.

I have wrapped my heart with so much passion
And put it in a sacred box for you
I have kissed your heart through your body and
Left the scent of love within
I have touched your sweet lips so gently that
It made me feel free and divine
Now I can speak so proudly because
Every cell of my body wants to dance.

"I love you, Marco," I said. I wanted to dance with him forever!

The night that I came back home from my trip with Marco, I packed and prepared everything for my drive to Northern California the next morning. It was already the second week of August and I was supposed to pick up Luka from Donna's house. He needed to get ready for his new school year which was about to start. It was around 6:00 a.m. that morning when I woke up with vaginal pain. I immediately got dressed and drove to the hospital. I was lying down on the exam table in the urgent care department and the doctor was doing a gynecology exam. She looked at me and told me that I had genital herpes caused by the herpes virus. She said that it was going to be very painful because she had to cut the blisters that had developed in order to drain them. I screamed loudly while the doctor cut the blisters. I was in terrible pain, but at the same time, I looked discombobulated and didn't understand what the doctor was saying. I asked her startlingly, "What do you mean I have genital herpes? I don't have any virus. That's impossible. Can you please explain it to me? What does it mean?" So, the doctor explained in detail what the herpes virus was. I was utterly lost and didn't believe that I had any virus; I was sure that I was healthy. But then she said that I could have contracted it from my partner if he had any blisters or sores anywhere while having sexual contact with me. Suddenly, I felt as if I had been struck by lightning when I recalled that Macro had a blister on his lip. He even poked the blister in the hotel bathroom the day we arrived at Laguna Beach. He told me that he hated when he got that blister and wanted to get rid of it. I shockingly said to the doctor, "Yes, he had a blister on his lip, but I didn't know it was the herpes virus. I thought it was just a blister, like a pimple. And then he burst it with a needle, and it was bleeding. Oh noooo . . ." The doctor shook her head and only thing she said was that the blister was herpes, and he shouldn't have burst it because he exposed me to it. I was speechless and disoriented. Later, in the hospital pharmacy, I picked up an antiviral medication that the doctor prescribed and went home.

I was already on my way, driving north, when Marco called and with a calm and sad voice, I told him everything. In truth, I wasn't angry at him, though I was lost and drained both physically and emotionally. For a few seconds, Marco was unable to get a word out. He was stunned by this revelation. He said that he had had that blister on and off since he was nineteen or twenty years old, and he never infected any woman in his entire life. He had many relationships and a wife for eight years and they were intimate even when he had the blister. As far as he knew, no one had ever gotten this from him and he had never believed that this blister was contagious.

He felt so horrible about it and kept apologizing to me, saying, "This is crazy! I wish you weren't driving. You should have stayed with me. I can't believe this . . . I am so sorry . . . so sorry."

I wanted to make it explicit and told him, "Marco, the blister on your lip that you said comes out in the sun is the herpes virus. It's a cold sore that's very contagious, and you can't have any oral contact when you have that sore. So, when you took that needle and burst open the blister, it released the virus and became highly contagious. I didn't know anything about herpes and cold sores. If I did, I would have protected myself and you too."

Marco was devastated. He agreed, "Of course, you're right, and the doctor is absolutely right. It is contagious, and I am *soooo stupid*. I wasn't thinking at the time. I have never infected any woman in my life. And because I've had this blister since I was very young, I didn't think that it would be contagious, and I wouldn't have wanted to infect anyone, especially you. You know how much I care about you, how much you mean to me, and how much I appreciate having you in my life. I never wanted to hurt you. If I had the tiniest thought at the moment that this blister would have been dangerous, I never would have had sex with you that night. But this was a pure mistake. I didn't think about it as a virus or something that was contagious and dangerous. *I would never ever harm you* . . . you know that. I am stupid. I am very stupid! I wish you weren't driving and had come to me after the doctor's appointment. I feel so terrible . . . I don't know what to say. *I am so sorry*, Russo. I feel so bad . . . *I am so sorry!*" I believed him. I knew Marco had never intended to do something like that, and it was just an unfortunate mistake on his part.

When I arrived at Donna's, they were all so excited to see me and I was relieved to finally get there. I missed my boy; he had grown so much during the summer. When I got inside the house, the dining table was set, and Donna had prepared my favorite dishes. She is a miracle woman! Although she is in a wheelchair, I still don't know how she does everything by herself—cooking, cleaning, and even gardening. And on top of that she's always been very positive and cheerful! Before I went to bed that night, I took another pill of the antiviral medication and then I left the bottle of medication on the guest bathroom counter; I forgot to put it back in my cosmetic bag. Donna rarely goes into that bathroom, unless she needs extra towels stored there. That night, unfortunately, she did. In the process, she discovered my medication on the bathroom counter. I was already in bed when Marco called and he sounded stressed and a little frightened. He asked me several times not to tell anyone about my diagnosis, and that this was our secret. He promised he would do everything to make sure that I was fine. I sensed Marco's emotions and told him, "Please, don't worry. Everything will be fine. I want you to be strong because that'll make me feel better and stronger."

There was a moment of silence and in a few seconds, Marco said with a firm voice, "Russo . . . *I will pay you!*" Then he stayed quiet. Those words had totally confused and shaken me. I replied, "What do you mean you will pay me? Pay me for what? For what happened to me? You think I want your money? You think I'm with you for your money? Marco, is that what you're thinking?"

Again, there was silence. I was getting even more confused and didn't understand what Marco meant about paying me. My voice started shaking. I was getting angry, and I said, "I want nothing from you. I will never take a penny from you. Do you hear me? I am with you because *I love you!*" I was feeling nauseous from the antiviral medication and told Marco that I didn't want to talk about anything anymore and had to go. He immediately stopped me and asked me to listen to him for a second. He said that he didn't mean that he would pay me money, but he would pay for the meds. That's what he meant. And he apologized if I understood it differently.

"Please know that I'm here for you, I care about you so much, and I'm very angry at myself. I'm so upset about this situation, and I don't know how to fix it. I know that I can't fix it, and that's killing me. Your love, graciousness, and kindness are killing me! I know how much you trusted me, and I let you down. I want to die and not hear all that. *Please forgive me . . . I'm sorry, I am very, very sorry.*" Marco was broken and distraught.

Before I hung up the phone, I said, "Marco, there is nothing to forgive because I don't blame you for this. I told you already, and I'll repeat myself again; this was just a mistake, and that's it. We all make mistakes, and I know it wasn't intentional. I believe one million percent that you never wanted to hurt me. I'll be fine, I promise. And right now, I don't need anything but thanks for your offer. I'm very tired and I have to go now. I'll talk to you tomorrow." I never blamed Marco for what I caught from him. I wholeheartedly believed that it was just a bad mistake and, for sure, I didn't want to watch how he suffered from this incident. I wanted to move on.

The next morning, it was around 8:00 a.m. when I received a call from my doctor's office. They had obtained my lab results and wanted to let me know that I had another bacterial infection that was caused by the open sores. I had to go to the pharmacy and fill the antibiotic prescription that my doctor gave me. I was still in bed, wasn't fully awake yet, and started reiterating quietly, "This is crazy . . . this is crazy! Oh nooo . . . this is crazy!" As soon as I hung up the phone, I saw that Marco had texted me several times: at midnight, 2:00 a.m., 6:00 a.m., and 7:00 a.m. I didn't feel up to reading any messages. I definitely didn't want Donna or Luka to notice that I wasn't feeling well or that I was hiding something from them. After breakfast, Luka and Hanley ran out into the backyard to play. I was helping Donna clean up the kitchen and that's when Donna asked me if I was OK. I replied that I was fine, but then she said she saw the antiviral medication on the counter in the bathroom and she knew what it was for. I felt bad that she had found out about it, but I also didn't want to lie to her and decided to share with her the truth. I told her that I contracted genital herpes from Marco, which I found out the day earlier—the same day I arrived at her house. With an upset voice, Donna asked me if Marco ever told me that he had the herpes virus. I said, "No, the only thing he mentioned a while back was that he has this blister that comes out on his lip once a year or every two years when he's out in the sun. Then he said he's had it since he was nineteen or twenty years old. And even when we were together in Laguna Beach, he told me that it wasn't contagious. So, I wasn't concerned at all because I thought it was just a pimple on his lip. I even felt like, who cares? That's fine. And then he burst it open with a needle in the bathroom. I had no clue about the herpes virus. I was absolutely sure that it was nothing. I'm so lost . . . and the only thing I know right now is that whatever I have is painful and extremely irritating."

Donna was getting very angry. "That fucking bastard! I'm sorry, honey . . . you know I don't speak like this in this house, but I am *very, very angry* at him! If he's had this blister since he was nineteen and now, he's fifty-four, right? Then he knows that this is herpes and that it is contagious! He's absolutely a fucking liar! And when he burst it with a needle and exposed it, then had sex with you, he infected you with it. He's a selfish and egotistical man! He knows that this is *contagious*. You are too naïve, honey. I feel horrible that you didn't know about it and he didn't have enough integrity, class, morality, or respect for you to protect you from this. If he really cared about you, he should have told you what he had without question!"

I got so emotional, and I was so tired of the whole thing. I asked Donna not to talk about Marco like that because he would've never wanted to hurt me; I trusted him on that. I told her that Marco made a *bad mistake* and that was it! I didn't feel well and wanted to throw up because the antiviral medication made me so sick. I thanked Donna for a lovely breakfast and went to my bedroom to lie down a little bit. I was overwhelmed.

It was early afternoon and Luka was at his best friend Sebastian's house, having a playdate. Donna was in the family room, reading the newspapers. I walked into the room and told her that I was going to the pharmacy to pick up my meds. I looked weary and pasty. She was very concerned about my appearance and looked furious. "I just want to *kill that man*! If this happened to me, I would have shot him for sure . . . that *bastard*! I can't believe you have a bacterial infection too. This summer has been just unbelievable for you. It's too much!" I told Donna, in a caring way, that Marco was devastated, and he wanted to die knowing what I was going through. "Let him die. Serves him right!" She replied and then continued, "He really showed how much he cared when he had sex with you with his exposed blister. And he told you that he takes medication for that blister, which means he knew what he had but he withheld that from you. That shows what a selfish and egotistical bastard he is. You're are too gracious! He's a lucky man that this happened to you and not to any other woman. And now you are telling me that he worries about you? He keeps calling and texting and checking on you and asking you not to tell anyone about this. I know why he's so terrified and what he's worried about, and why he doesn't want you to tell anyone anything. Let me tell you this. If this happened to me, I would have shot him—I told you that earlier—and a certain percentage of women would have done the same. But some women would have destroyed him differently by suing him. That would serve him right because he's an egotistical liar, sitting on his pedestal, and what he did is immoral, unethical, and illegal. Don't forget that he is a wealthy and successful man. He would pay anything—any amount—not to ruin his reputation and career. That's what he cares about the most! So, these women would have fucked him over financially and would have walked away from him forever, no question about it! Sorry for my language but I think there is only one person who would have accepted this so lovingly and graciously, and that's you, honey, and I don't know how you're doing it. *This is killing me!* And now you're worried about him? Let him die, let him break down, and let him go crazy! Who cares?"

"*I care*," I replied in a firm and low tone. "We all make mistakes, and I think we should be forgiven for our mistakes. We should learn from them and move on. I know Marco made a terrible mistake, and he suffers from that. I can feel his devastation and regret. But I want to move on and continue this relationship with him because I love him. I believe in him, and I know that he has a wonderful heart and soul. And I know that he loves me too. I've already accepted what I got from him because this is the only way I can move on and leave the past behind. I hope Marco can forgive himself and accept what happened so he can move on too. You know that our connection ever since we met is like nothing I've ever experienced before. Even with my children's fathers I didn't have this intensity of emotion. Right from the very beginning, it was like Marco and I were destined to be together. We both instantly bonded and felt like we had known each other for years. Maybe we did in another life . . . who knows? This isn't just a fleeting love affair . . . I'm convinced that we're soul mates on this journey together."

"Are you nuts?" asked Donna. I totally understood where her frustration and anger were coming from because she loves and cares about me so much. And she wasn't only concerned about my health, but she also wanted to protect me like every good parent wants to protect his or her loved ones. But I asked her that day to support me in whatever decision I made in my life. I also asked her to try to forgive Marco and not to talk about him like that because I believed that would have been better for all of us. And most of all, I needed to get over the side effects of the antiviral medication and heal myself. I just needed some solitude.

I spoke with Marco later that day and explained to him that Donna accidently saw the antiviral medication in my bathroom and she knew what it was for. Therefore, I told her what happened. He hated to hear that and sounded overwrought. He wanted to call Donna and apologize and even wanted to go and see her in person. But I said that it wasn't a good idea to speak with her. Everyone needed some time to get over this initial shock.

After Luka and I returned home from Donna's, it was one of the nights when Marco stayed with us. Luka was already in bed and Marco and I were having tea in the kitchen. He was sitting at the table, looking very sad and depressed with his head hung in shame; he couldn't even look at me. He was hardly breathing. He said that he couldn't sleep at night thinking about this and how much he hurt me. And while I was gone, he was crying every single day. I sat on his lap and embraced him; he embraced me back and started sobbing. I said that he was my sweet Marco and I loved him. He abruptly got up and pulled me from his lap. He got even madder and more frustrated when he felt the love that I had for him. He was still scared about what he had done. "Your love is killing me!" Marco said loudly with mixed emotions. "What makes you say you love me? Maybe a couple of months from now you'll wake up, realize the severity of what happened, and hate me for this. Maybe right now you're blinded by love, and you don't see the gravity of the situation. If you were screaming and telling me that you hate me, it'd be a more natural and realistic reaction." I was standing and listening to him calmly. I felt his frightful feelings of annoyance and disappointment. I said that I accepted whatever I got from him with love, and I wasn't going to hate or yell at him because of his mistake. I trusted and believed in him. Marco didn't tell me what he had because he wanted to hurt me, *absolutely not*, there is no question about that. He never wanted to infect me with this virus. I believe the reason that he didn't disclose that he had this virus was because he was ignorant and unconscious like *I* was in those days and he neither loved nor accepted himself the way he was. The same can be said about me.

Perhaps this relationship was important to both of us, for our individual reasons. I can't speak for him, but I can speak for myself. Today I am convinced that the central message of this connection between Marco and me was that he had to teach me something in this lifetime. There was something very fundamental to be discovered in the course of our relationship. Lessons come in a variety of forms, and I believe the core lesson that I needed to learn through this connection was how to speak up and say the truth and how to love and accept myself.

⚬⚭⚬

The medication that I had taken for the herpes outbreaks had given me terrible side effects. There were only two main antiviral meds for this virus, and my doctor prescribed the other one in September 2017, when I got my outbreaks again.

I was driving home from the hospital when Marco called and asked me if I got the meds and the prescription cream from the pharmacy. I replied that I got a different antiviral medication but not the cream and didn't say why. He insisted, "I don't understand you. What's wrong with you? Why don't you want to get the cream? You should be trying everything to feel better. What's the big deal about getting a cream for your outbreaks?" Then I replied that the prescription cream cost almost four hundred dollars and my insurance didn't cover it. I had to pay for it out of pocket, and I couldn't spend that kind of money just for that tiny tube. Marco got angry; he told me that I was crazy for not telling him that. He said he would pay for the cream, and he would give me the money the next time that he saw me. And then in a few seconds, he added, "If you feel uncomfortable taking my money perhaps you can make soup for me. No . . . you always cook for me. You don't need to do that. Hmm . . . you can buy me a gift instead, or this will be my gift to you. All right?" After hearing all this from him, I was dazed. I felt very awkward after listening to Marco. I paused, then said, "You don't need to give me money, but I will always make soup for you. Let's not talk about this anymore." Marco sensed that I didn't like his comments, and he started laughing. He said that he was joking about it and couldn't wait to see me.

❧

One of the early afternoons a few weeks later, I was nauseous and dizzy from the meds and was lying down on my bed.

Luka was at school and I was by myself at home. I got a little scared and called Donna. I told her that I was getting side effects from the other medication, too, and wasn't feeling well. She suggested that I call my doctor and get her advice about continuing the meds. Then she asked if Marco was helping me and if he gave me the money for the cream when he came to visit us over the weekend. "No, he forgot. But he always offers his help and asks me if I need anything," I replied.

"And . . . what's your response?" Donna tried to imitate my voice, "*No, thank you, I have everything I need.*' So, he conveniently forgot to pay for the cream that you need because of his irresponsibility? This is bullshit! Sorry, honey, but I don't care anymore. He is so fucking wealthy . . . He's driving a half-million-dollar Ferrari, but he can't pay four hundred dollars for the cream? He is *soooo* cheap! Instead of coming once a week to your place, he should be there all the time, doing errands, grocery shopping, helping with Luka, and even cooking. You always cook for him! Has he ever picked up dinner for you in the past four months while you were so sick you couldn't even get out of your place? *No!* Has he ever come with you to the hospital when you ended up in the ER and urgent care twenty-five times in the past four months? *No!* Only once has he taken you there, and that's a big deal? Has he ever asked you how much medical expense you've incurred in the past few months? Of course not! Does he understand how difficult it is for a single mom to raise a child under normal circumstances, let alone with unexpected medical bills? He doesn't care! Otherwise, he would have just done what needed to be done, whether you asked him to or not!" Donna's voice was rising up. She was getting exceedingly furious. "You were unable to focus on your work or do anything for the past four months because of him. For God's sake, you had a catheter for an entire month, and you were still grocery shopping and cooking for him! Russo, *what's wrong with you?* You need to love yourself first, take care of yourself, and think about yourself! Let him buy his own goddamn soup and dinner! You are making everything so easy for him. That's not right. Marco doesn't deserve a woman like you. He's in love with his money and himself and is afraid to spend a penny if it doesn't benefit him. Honey, you're a gracious, beautiful, intelligent, and generous woman and you deserve so much better—*so much better*! If I were you, I would've hired a lawyer and sued the shit out of him . . . That's what he deserves. What a selfish, greedy bastard!" Donna, like my mother, has always been there for me and in those days, she tried to wake me up in her own unique way, but I still didn't want to hear all of that from her. I never wanted to hurt Marco, nor did I want his money. The only thing I wanted from him was his love and for him to be more responsible and considerate. I had gotten introspective and thought, *Maybe I should have asked him for things. Maybe that was my mistake, thinking that he would do it on his own.* I was in tears and in pain. I didn't know what I was doing wrong.

❦

It was Marco's stepfather Carlos's birthday. Marco and I were with him in a restaurant to celebrate his special day together.

Carlos was so content and cheerful having both of us there with him. The restaurant had a singer with a live band and after some time, they began the song "I Just Called to Say I Love You" by Stevie Wonder. Marco grabbed my hand and we both headed to the dance floor. While dancing, Marco sang along and at the end, he said, "I love you, Russo." This was the first time he ever told me that he loved me. I was so thrilled to hear that from him. But in the next instant he quickly added, "I love you, but don't be excited. I'm not there yet, but I'm getting there." Within a second, my exhilaration vanished. But I didn't want to spoil Marco's father's birthday so I kept smiling and dancing even though I was really *hurt*. After dinner, Marco brought me home and before I got out of the car, I told him that his comment "I love you, but don't be excited. I'm not there yet, but I'm getting there" made me feel like I needed to work harder to deserve his love. I didn't understand what he meant about me not getting excited. I asked, "What was that all about? That comment was very upsetting and hurtful. If you're not sure about your feelings, about whether you love me, then don't say anything until you are! Nobody asked you to say it. I was so happy to hear it from you at that perfect moment while we were dancing, but you spoiled it completely. When I say 'I love you,' it comes from my heart and soul so naturally and easily. I don't need to think about it . . . I just feel it. Please don't hurt me with comments like that again." He apologized and conceded that it wasn't the right thing to say. He sounded embarrassed and didn't know what to say. Then he hugged and kissed me.

I kissed him back and said, "Love you."

"I love you, too . . . but I'm not *in love with you,*" Marco responded. I looked at him, paused, and then faintly smiled. I got out of the car and said good night. *And that night was our last night together.* The next morning, I was so sick, depressed, and wrecked that I couldn't get up to take Luka to school. My eyes were red and swollen and Luka had never seen me like that before. He was very concerned and scared because of the way I looked. I told him that I was fine and that he needed to walk to school quickly before he was late. Shortly after I got up, I sat down at my desk, turned the computer on, and wrote a farewell letter to Marco, penning my final goodbye to him.

"Dear Marco,

I am writing this letter with much love. After our conversation yesterday, I had a wake-up call, and I was awake all night, thinking about our relationship. The one thing that I finally understand is that I'm with a man who loves and cares about me as a friend but who is truly not in love with me. If these past eight months are any indication of your true feelings for me then you'll never fall in love with me. I remember so clearly on our third date that you told me the following: "I don't believe it when people say it takes time to fall in love with a person, like after five or six months you've had enough time, and by

then you should be in love with your partner.
It doesn't work like that for me. Either I fall in
love with a woman right in the beginning or
I never do."

These are your true words! I don't want or
need that kind of relationship. It's not healthy
or fair for either of us—and especially not for
my son. I'm a responsible mother raising a
teenager, and I can't deal with a casual relationship. This is definitely not what I want.
I know that the last four months have been
extremely emotional for both of us, and I
think now it's time for me to think rational-
ly and focus on healing myself. One thing I
want you to know is that my feelings for you
have always been very strong and genuine,
and I want you to find the same thing with
someone that you can fall in love with. I'm
very thankful for the memories that we created together and especially grateful for finally
knowing how to accept and love myself first
and foremost. As Rumi said in one of his poems, "He said, 'How do you benefit from this
life?' / I said, 'By keeping true to myself.'"
At last, I want to be true to myself just as I
want to have peace, bliss, and harmony. And
I want the same for you. It's been extremely
difficult for me to write this farewell letter, but
I know this is the right thing to do in order for

both of us to move on. I hope you'll find love
and happiness in the future.

Love,
Russo"

It was devilishly painful to let him go but I was sure that
it was the right thing to do. The irony is that I met Marco
in February 2017 with his stepfather at the same restaurant
where we actually celebrated his stepfather's birthday, and
our relationship ended there that night, eight months later.
You may be curious to know if Marco ever replied to my
letter—no, he never did.

The journey with Marco took me into a dark labyrinth where
our relationship unfolded the hidden strength in me that I
never would have found without him. Being with Marco felt
as if I was on a roller coaster with lots of highs and lows.
There were days full of love, connection, warmth, and joy,
and there were days of disappointments, sadness, and tears.

With Erekle, my heart was broken while I was with him
but when I separated from him, honestly, I was relieved. With
Giorgi, on the other hand, my heart used to break every time
I saw him drunk and watched how he suffered from his addic-
tion. When I broke up with him, I was very sad and shattered.
However, after breaking up with Marco, my heart opened up.
As Rumi said, "You have to keep breaking your heart until

it opens." To be specific, I didn't become stronger or honest with myself or others when I let my heart become cold and closed in the aftermath of disappointments or heartbreaks. It was only when I fully surrendered and accepted the process of grieving for my broken heart that I realized those painful experiences that I encountered on my path finally opened my heart, broadened my understanding, and guided me to the truth that I was seeking for such a long time.

As far as love is concerned, I loved all three of those men in my own way, otherwise I would not have chosen to be with them. What those relationships taught me was that it wasn't about the first, second, or last love, but it was about the experiences that made me start loving myself first.

After breaking up with Marco, I was in an excruciating pain, thinking those days would never pass and that pain would remain with me forever. I couldn't stop crying for fourteen months and I grieved for two years. But what I was actually lamenting for then wasn't the breakup with Marco, but for not being able to be truthful with him and, most importantly, with myself. Ultimately, the uncommunicated truth that I had suppressed inside me wanted to come out; it was fed up with being ignored and restrained.

When you burn wood in a fireplace, the fire is strong and intense in the beginning, but then slowly it weakens and vanishes, though the ashes that are scattered will remain in the fireplace until you remove them. If you keep the ashes for a long time, it can cause serious health effects. I can compare my first two relationships with my former spouses to a burning log that turned into ashes at the end. But instead of discarding the ashes and treasuring my learnings from those relationships, by accepting my sorrows, fears, and pain, I buried those acidic ashes deep within me. I wasn't dead inside yet and was unable to rise from the ashes, like a phoenix. However, my relationship with Marco not only provoked me to die inside and slowly burn out as a log in a fireplace but also hastened my rebirth as a new person with true self—the self that was awakened, enough, and whole; the self that no longer searched for love outside and was willing to turn the flames of suffering into understanding and change. If we bury all of our wounds within us and ignore them, thinking that time will heal them, eventually we will understand that time doesn't heal our pain. Only we can heal it if we allow ourselves to face, acknowledge, and accept it. We have all heard the saying that *time heals everything.*

In the latter part of our relationship, Marco had shared with me more details about his early years. And now I acknowledge how Marco's childhood experiences had both hardened and wounded him at the same time. He had lost trust in the most trustworthy person that a child could ever have—his mother—when he was only a little boy. He grew up with the fear that his mom might come into his room one night and kill him. Marco's mother was very young when her husband abandoned the two of them and that devastated her. Therefore, she frequently used to take her anger out on Marco by verbally abusing and threatening him. Marco had never known what real, unconditional love was. He never felt it as a child and, as a result, in his adult years, he didn't know how to *give it* either. Despite that, he wanted love so much, he yearned it and searched for it outside, like me. Even though I kept avoiding men for years after every heartbreaking encounter that I had faced on my path, deep inside, my heart longed for love. Unlike Marco, I was raised in one of the most loving families that I could've ever asked for. Despite that, during the course of my journey, I still needed to learn one of the most fundamental human necessities, which is *self-love*. So, in essence, my relationship with Marco on some level continued to remind me of the inner conflicts that I hadn't resolved in my life because of my ego, which kept me quiet and untruthful to myself and to him. Getting beyond the stage of resentment or blame to the stage of self-reflection was a vital step for me to take, yet it took me more than two decades before I began to realize that I didn't come here to change or fix anyone; it was *me* who needed to change. Today, I know for sure that I came here to love, forgive, and support others as well as to heal and to be healed. Nothing that transpired in my life was without a perfect and loving purpose and everything is as it should be.

⚬⚬⚬

I was a slow learner irrespective of being surrounded by great role models who tried to assist and guide me throughout my journey. It took me so much time, many efforts, and lots of failures to learn and grow by myself. Many times, in my relationships, I ignored the crucial signs that required my attention, so that ignorance led me all the way down to the bottom of my own darkness where I not only had to face my own fears, insecurities, and shadows but also accept and surrender to them before finding my way back into the light. When you silence the truth repeatedly, it will keep appearing and rising to the surface until it wakes you up and gets your full attention.

In order to find the path of truth, I needed to go through the dark woods, like Dante Alighieri, Italian poet and philosopher, described in *Inferno*: "I came to myself within a dark wood where the straight way was lost." I had to face the darkness on my path, where I knew that there was no turning back; going through it was the only option. It was excruciating and arduous—*nothing like a fairy tale*—but it was a journey that I had chosen, and I had to find my own strength and the hidden tools to help me find what I was looking for. What I was seeking was nowhere else but inside me. It was my *soul, my true self.* Yet me acknowledging the truth didn't come without consequences; eventually, I broke down completely. In fact, I needed to break down in order to wake up and hear the eternal music that my soul was playing for me all of these years—the music of truth, which I had never heard until then. Carl Jung said, "There is no coming to consciousness without pain."

Honestly, until now, I would have never imagined going back and reawakening all of those miserable, disappointing, and tormenting days that I experienced in the past with my relationships. But currently, I'm so grateful for diving deep and getting to the root of the pain from all of those years. In the past, I concealed the basis of that pain so deep within myself that I could never find it. Oftentimes, my internal pain wanted to communicate with me, but I ignored it because of my fearful mind, and I had no desire to feel it again. However, writing this book gave me an opportunity to dig deep within myself to become an observer of my own thoughts and actions. Since every pain has a story, and it needs a good listener to become the healer of that pain. Once I recognized and acknowledged my pain, it became so much easier to let the pain go with love and compassion and allowed me to be my own healer, since I wasn't avoiding or escaping from it any longer. There were no wrong paths; there were paths that I was meant to be on. I kept facing those tumultuous experiences until I ultimately opened up to them. Undeniably, those experiences were part of my unrepeatable journey on earth and, today, I am thankful for them because I chose them, was responsible for them, and most of all, I eventually learned from them. As opposed to victimizing myself, I want to turn my road of tribulations into a road of learning, opportunity, growth, and transformation. And if there is anyone in this world to blame for continuously bearing the pain and silencing the truth, it could be only one person, and *that's me.*

Blaming myself for my past occurrences and mistakes would trap me in the past forever, and from now on I don't want to live there any longer. I was lost then and was unaware of myself when I was used by my past memories and painful encounters. Today, I choose to be more present, practice awareness, live consciously and appreciate what each day brings to me—a new life, a new knowledge, a new opportunity. And I am willing to use all of the tools that I've discovered within me to create a better future. It's never too late to change and begin a new chapter to open a new door. I have no doubt that whatever experiences I had endured were part of my journey and whoever crossed my path came as a guide to help me reach my fullest potential so I can become who and what I really am. "Be grateful for whoever comes, because each has been sent as a guide from beyond."—Rumi

I wrote the following poem in 2019 while I was in the process of searching for answers:

> *I've questioned myself*
> *So many times.*
> *Where did I make a mistake?*
> *Or didn't do it right?*
> *How could I have done things differently*
> *To avoid the pain, disappointments, and*
> *Heartbreaks throughout my life?*
> *So, one day, I was sitting*
> *In an easy pose, breathing quietly*
> *And then I closed my eyes.*
> *After a long silence and stillness,*
> *The answer crossed my mind.*
> *I did nothing wrong—*
> *This is just my journey on earth*
> *And my unrepeatable life.*

One of the key points that I want to share with you is that I had a secret guilt that I carried since my childhood and never talked about it until after my breakup with Marco. When I was a little girl, my father used to tell me, "Don't ever choose a man just because he's wealthy, nor ask a man, when you start dating, to buy you expensive gifts or spend money on you. Don't love money! Love your family, your country, and people. I provide everything for you, and I'm raising you to be a proper, upstanding, and intelligent girl. Never lose your integrity, morals, and class and don't forget where you come from." Those were the words that I always remembered, though I interpreted them in an erroneous way. After breaking up with my boyfriend, I blamed my father's words imprinted in my memories. I always felt awkward and ashamed to ask a man with whom I had a relationship, for anything. I avoided even to the simplest things—for instance, picking up meds for me from the pharmacy or buying yogurt, strawberries, or chocolate. But then I realized I would remain trapped in pain and unhappiness as long as I kept blaming my father for something that truly didn't exist. It wasn't his fault that I couldn't ask for things. It was my *ego* that kept me locked into fears for all of these years, and for that reason, I felt ashamed to ask my boyfriend for anything. The voice in my head continued to say, *You are a strong, independent, smart woman. You can take care of yourself, and you don't need to bother your boyfriend.* So, instead of blaming my dad for all of that, I finally spoke up and told him what was troubling me all of these years. That is, the belief that he inscribed on my mind about men. As I was speaking with him over the phone, I poured out my resentment, sorrows, and confusion and I burst into tears as I told him how I felt. This was the first time in my entire life when I felt so vulnerable while speaking with my father so unashamedly and honestly. I was sobbing and told him,

"When I was sick, I couldn't ask my boyfriend to go to the pharmacy to pick up my meds and then to get dinner for three of us yet the worst part was that he never considered doing it by himself. I wasn't asking him for diamond earrings or a five-thousand-dollar dress! I remember that my mom didn't need to ask you for things. When she was sick, you automatically did everything for her." My father was listening to me so quietly that, at first, I thought the call disconnected. But he was there—silent—and I heard a long, deep sigh of sadness. He was heartbroken hearing my devastating voice and emotions. After a massive outpouring of confession, my father at last spoke up and said, "My dear, you deserve everything. Not only love, care, respect, and appreciation of a man, but all kinds of diamonds, the most elegant dresses, and everything precious that exists in this universe; however, that man wasn't worthy of a woman like you and one who deserves you will not make you suffer and cry like this." His words instantaneously soothed me, and I felt so much love flowing throughout my body. All of these years, I had never spoken up and discussed my personal issues and problems with my dad so boldly and genuinely. The pain that consumed me finally broke me open and enabled me to show my real self to my dad, revealing the secret guilt about him that I carried throughout my childhood.

❦

My mother and other incredible women who crossed my path came into my life to empower me and be my voice when I felt voiceless. They gave me the strength when I felt powerless and saw me as being worthy when I felt worthless. However, today by sharing my story, I want to be a voice of other girls and women who feel just the way I felt in those days. Certainly, there are millions of girls and women throughout the world who don't have parents like I have and have no one to rely on to feel safe or protected. They face violence, discrimination, and injustice every day of their lives. In spite of the fact that I had my parents who always had my back, I still needed to find my voice on my own, along my path. It was *fear* that disempowered me, held me back, and tried to disable me to find my voice and kept me silent, away from the truth. Sometimes, silence can be a lifesaver and it can be the best answer, but on the contrary, silence can also be deadly. Having a voice is crucial and having the ability and courage to stand up for ourselves is indispensable. And remember, "No one saves us, but ourselves. No one can and no one may. We ourselves must walk the path."—Buddha

Every girl and woman in this world has all of these qualities: strength, courage, inner power, wisdom, values, and unlimited abilities; they only need to believe in themselves, find those gifts and traits within them, and dare to find the strength to speak up. *Speak up . . . speak up . . . Please speak up for yourself, be brave, because no one can do it for you, no matter how hard they try.* Once we speak up, our angels and invisible helpers are always there to help, protect, and guide us. They want us to change and evolve.

Throughout my life, women have verily continued to uplift and support me. But it is men who have been my greatest teachers, who have challenged me to learn and grow emotionally, spiritually, and intellectually, and they came into my life to awaken me from the fear and illusion that I lived in for such a long time. It is men who taught me the most valuable lesson in the art of loving, accepting, and forgiving myself and others. They confronted me causing me to ultimately speak the truth and find my voice.

It took me so long, more than two decades, to finally recognize that I have a *voice*. What we all have is *our voice*. We came here with a purpose and we are free to have a voice. Let's use it, let's speak up, no matter how hard it is; it is even harder when you stay silent and unheard. And remember you are not alone; *we are all in this together.*

❦

Mark Twain once said, "The two most important days in your life are the day you are born and the day you find out why."

Now I would say the two dearest countries in my life are the country of Georgia, where I was *born*, and the United States of America, where I *found myself.*

Throughout my childhood, my birth country taught me how to sow the seeds of love and hospitality and humbleness and kindness and generosity and how to carry those seeds along my journey. But the United States of America helped me find the light in everything—in despair, anger, pain, adversity, and failure. America laid its wing as a bridge to me and allowed me to join its choir that performs the music of freedom and democracy, equality and bravery, love and peace. Therefore, I will forever be indebted to both countries for their lifelong lessons and guidance.

Last but not least, I want to devote the final chapter of this book to the historic event that we have all been confronting together since 2020—the COVID-19 pandemic.

29

CORONAVIRUS EPIDEMIC
LOS ANGELES (2020)

As I am writing this book, we all are experiencing the most scary, chaotic, and nerve-racking time throughout the world. The 2019–2020 coronavirus outbreak is part of everyone's life. We aren't facing this challenge alone. Since we are all in this together, I'd like to share with you my personal vignettes as to how I faced these trying days, especially in the beginning.

In the early morning of March 19, 2020, I was standing in one of those long lines outside of a small grocery store where almost everyone was protecting themselves and others by wearing the masks, gloves, and other protective gear. What I sensed while standing in the line for a tolerable amount of time was that stillness and silence prevailed among every single person. Then, as small groups of patrons were allowed entrance into the store, the same calmness continued. The interior of the store was spotless, impeccably organized, and all of the goods were shining so brightly that it seemed like they were polished. As I was shopping, it was the first time that I noticed how every customer, including me, was present and aware of the surroundings. I felt that people were shopping consciously and appreciating everything that was available in the store, because I was doing the same thing. I was grateful that they had every product that I needed that day. I was thanking God quietly with these words: "God, thank you. Thank you for everything that is here right now." Customers were also mindful of the employees and were thanking them for keeping the store stocked and sanitary, and for their bravery for working. Almost a week earlier, on March 13, 2020, when the national emergency was declared in the United States, I happened to be in one of the larger retail stores in the city. What I experienced that day was exceptionally unexpected and shocking. Everyone was panicking and grabbing as many toilet paper rolls and water bottles as were accessible. It is impossible to not overreact when you are in the middle of such collective chaos. On that day, I wasn't in the store for toilet paper or for water. I needed just a few grocery products but the anxiety in the shop was extremely overwhelming. So, I automatically grabbed a case of water and put it into my cart. Next, I started walking towards the other aisles and when I reached the toilet paper section, all of the shelves were emptied out. The canned foods and pasta shelves were cleared out as well. At first, I was more disoriented than frightened and was lost in the moment of observing how the racks were emptying out so quickly. Products from every aisle that I walked through—frozen food, dairy, meat produce, and sundries—were disappearing so fast that I didn't have time to process everything or even be scared because I didn't have time to *think*. I just continued staring at the cleared shelves in amazement. At that moment, there was a middle-aged woman who was standing next to me in one of those aisles. She was terribly anxious and said out loud, "This is so scary." Instantaneously I replied to her, "Don't worry, everything will be just fine."

I don't know what made me say those words to that lady, but in that moment, although most of the shelves were wiped out, I still remained positive and felt that I needed to say something supportive and reassuring to her with a warm smile. She glanced at me and then walked away quietly, with no comment. After a little pause, the first thought that came alarmingly into my mind was, *Go and get some bread before it's all gone; you have no bread at home.* I promptly pushed my cart and headed to the bread aisle. In the meantime, my childhood memories sprang to my mind. As you'll recall, during the nineties in Georgia, we had huge bread and water lines and they were imprinted on my mind. People were especially desperate to buy a sufficient amount of bread for their families. In those days, while I saw those disorganized and messy lines, I never stood in them. And as a young girl, I feared nothing, though my parents and grandparents did stand in those unbearable lines to get bread for their loved ones. They worried tremendously about the unstable life and hardship that we were enduring. Consequently, as this memory resurfaced to me in the market that day, I knew it was my turn to protect my family by getting some groceries and enough bread. The voice in my head kept repeating, *You can't eat the toilet paper so get bread and the things that you can eat.* Therefore, I quickly reached the baking aisle and as you would've expected, all shelves were cleared out. Suddenly, in the corner, I noticed a rack where only three honey baguettes were left. As I got closer to it, I saw there were two young ladies standing there and they weren't sure whether to purchase the baguettes or not. They asked me if I had ever tasted that bread before. I looked at the baguette and replied, "I've never tasted this baguette before; however, now we have a chance to get and try it. It could have a little honey sweetness, but *who cares?* There is no other bread left in the store!" We all swiftly grabbed one each and exchanged smiles.

"We are not human beings having a spiritual experience. We are spiritual beings having a human experience." Many of us have heard these words from the French philosopher, Pierre Teilhard de Chardin. I believe that we are eternal souls where unconditional love and compassion, peace and kindness dwell. We all need food, water, and other basic needs to survive in this world and that moment in the market was a true example of having *a human experience.* That moment also made me realize how blessed and fortunate we are because we are all here on this planet together and we have this rare opportunity to experience this unrepeatable, unique time in human history. What I've learned from all of my experiences is that only arduous times can help us grow and learn. Particularly in these most challenging and trying times while fear and despair, pain and loss are escalating, the entire world is united. In fact, these tormenting and highly chaotic times teach us the most valuable lessons. The only thing we need to do is to ask questions about this life. What is it that you want to teach me now? What can I learn from these experiences? How can I use this time to become healthier, stronger, and more helpful, compassionate, and conscious? Our souls are hungry and eager to expand and learn from these experiences but if we are stuck in a painful place where our destructive ego is in full control and keeps us unconscious, then we will remain the victims not of the conditions or circumstances that we are in but the victims of our own resentful, fearful, and limited thoughts. We can only perceive and appreciate the light when we experience darkness and that thought brings me back to my own teenage years in Georgia. When we had a civil war from 1991–1993, the entire country was out of power for months on end during those years. I recall so perfectly when the dark streets and houses lighted up in our neighborhood and after we had electricity restored for just a few hours, it was gone again. But while we had power, everyone jumped with joy. The kids were exhilarated, and people recognized the full worth of the power of light. It felt like we all got our lives back. In truth, we can find the light in everything, in despair and failure, loss and anger and pain and celebrate it the way we rejoiced the restoration of light after we encountered so much darkness.

This notable time of history once again proves that we are not separated, unrelated, or different from one another; we are deeply connected with our ancestors and their ancestors and we are part of each other's lives. As Mother Teresa said, "If we have no peace, it is because we have forgotten that we belong to each other." We came here as tree branches to touch other branches with love, kindness, and compassion, no matter from where our roots originate.

Indeed, this book gave me an incredible opportunity to share with you the journey that I have been navigating all of these years and the experiences that showered me with the two most valuable gifts—to *forgive* and *love* myself and others. If I can love myself with all of my flaws and imperfections then I can love others with their shortcomings, and I can also allow others to love and accept me *the way I am*.

I would like to close this final chapter with the most powerful and magical words: *Thank you* for all those who presented me with all the experiences and blessings I've encountered in my life. *Thank you* for all of the blessings I am receiving now and I'm going to receive in the future. Most of all, *thank you*, my dear reader, for taking your precious time to read about my life story.

THANK YOU!

ACKNOWLEDGMENTS

There aren't enough words to adequately express my gratitude to Cynthia Martin for inspiring me to write and bring *A Hummingbird's Awakening* into existence. Thank you, Cynthia, for this invaluable gift!

Great thanks are due to Palmetto Publishing Group for their diligent, professional, and thorough work. It is a joy to work with you all.

I've been blessed and gifted with two exceptionally amazing and strong women:

Donna O'Connor and my mother, Lali, who made this whole process so delightful and easy. Thank you! Thank you! Thank you!

Love and gratitude to my beloved family: my sons, Chiko and Luka; my father, Shalva; my brother, Lasha, and his wife, Elena.

I am deeply thankful to a divine power: God, my universe, my invisible helpers, and angels, as well as all of the spiritual teachers, motivational speakers, and authors (to whom I referred in this book), whose teachings guided and assisted me through their books and writings and whose wisdom and strength throughout this long creative endeavor helped me bring this book to fruition.

Lastly, this book wouldn't have been possible without those people who crossed my path and came into my life as *a guide from beyond.*

ABOUT THE AUTHOR

Growing up in the country of Georgia, Russo began her passion for writing by expressing her thoughts, dreams, and goals in her simple childhood diary, which she has retained to this day. By writing stories and poetries from a very young age, she became an adventurer, taking on different personas and experiencing the heartache and happiness of the human spirit through the written word. Russo earned a BA in Mass Media Studies and Television Broadcasting at the University of Westminster in London and that catapulted her into international television broadcasting and production. Her exposure to European culture and customs provided a foundation for her creativity but her dreams only began being truly fulfilled after she established her home in the US and published her poetry collection, titled *A Hummingbird's Reminder*, and her debut novel, *A Hummingbird's Nest*. Her latest production, published in 2020, is an audio poetry book titled *Poems by Russo Shanidze*.

ENDNOTES

1   Lumiere Energy Healing. "Cynthia Martin." https://lumier-eenergyhealing.com

2   Tolle, Eckhart. "The End of Suffering." *YouTube* video, 5:14. April 12, 2008. https://www.youtube.com/watch?v=Deq_llg-9Dlo

3   Wikipedia. "Georgia (country)," May 10, 2021. https://en.wikipedia.org/wiki/Georgia_(country)

4   Wikipedia. "Georgian Language," May 6, 2021. https://en.wikipedia.org/wiki/Georgian_language

5   Wikipedia. "Georgian Civil War," April 27, 2021. https://en.wikipedia.org/wiki/Georgian_Civil_War).

6   Wines of Georgia, 2021. https://winesgeorgia.com/winemaking-tradition/

7   All Poetry. "The Moon over Mtatsminda." https://allpoetry.com/The-Moon-over-Mtatsminda

8   Jean Houston, *The Wizard of Us: Transformational Lessons from Oz.* (New York, NY: Atria Paperback, a Division of Simon & Schuster, Inc., 2012), p.52.

9   Wikipedia. "Ashdod," May 12, 2021. https://en.wikipedia.org/wiki/Ashdod

10   MatrixOxirtaM. "Wayne Dyer - How to Be a No-Limit Person." *YouTube* video, 1:05:28. April 27, 2012. https://www.youtube.com/watch?v=YjhTlYfLQGk&t=1629s

11   Dr. Joe Dispenza, *The Balance Between Intention and Surrender,*

January 19, 2018, https://blog.drjoedispenza.com/blog/mastery/the-balance-between-intention-and-surrender

12   Tolle, Eckhart. "How Do I Respond to Another's Pain-Body?" *YouTube* video, 7:03. May 9, 2013. https://www.youtube.com/watch?v=AcYrm7h86Rk

13   Mace, Lilou. "Gary Zukav: How to Create Authentic Power? Love vs. Fear." *YouTube* video, 45:06. June 10, 2011. https://www.youtube.com/watch?v=GAhw--24t1g&t=1458s

14   Mace, Lilou. "Gary Zukav: How to Create Authentic Power? Love vs. Fear." *YouTube* video, 45:06. June 10, 2011. https://www.youtube.com/watch?v=GAhw--24t1g&t=1458s

15   James Allen, *As A Man Thinketh*, (First Published in 1903 by James Allen. Reprint edition by Sound Wisdom, 2019). p. 61.

16   Wikipedia. "Matthew 7:7–8," in the King James Version of the Bible, February 25, 2021. https://en.wikipedia.org/wiki/Matthew_7:7–8

17   Jean Houston, *The Wizard of Us*: *Transformational Lessons from Oz*. (New York, NY: Atria Paperback, a Division of Simon & Schuster, Inc., 2012), p.151.

18   Zukav, Gary. "Addiction and Spiritual Growth." *YouTube* video, 5:01. February 12, 2015. https://www.youtube.com/watch?v=jKwNKfwTp-k

19   Eckhart Tolle, *The Power of Now*: *A Guide to Spiritual Enlightenment*. (Novato, CA: New World Library and Vancouver, B.C., Canada: Namaste Publishing Inc., 1997), p. 229.

20   Wikipedia. "Istanbul," May 15, 2021. https://en.wikipedia.org/wiki/Istanbul

21   Wikipedia. "*Vremya*," April 17, 2021. https://en.wikipedia.org/wiki/Vremya

22   Wikipedia. "Rustavi 2," April 23, 2021. https://en.wikipedia.org/wiki/Rustavi_2

23   Wikipedia. "Turtle Lake (Tbilisi)," April 18, 2021. https://en.wikipedia.org/wiki/Turtle_Lake_(Tbilisi)

24   Wikipedia. "Akhaltsikhe," April 15, 2021. https://en.wikipedia.org/wiki/Akhaltsikhe

25   Marianne Williamson, *A Return to Love: Reflections on the Principles of A Course in Miracles*. (HarperCollins Publishers Inc., 1992), p.117.

26   Elizabeth Lesser, *Broken Open: How Difficult Times Can Help Us Grow*. (Penguin Random House LLC, New York. 2004-2005), p.10,11.

27   Elizabeth Lesser, *Broken Open: How Difficult Times Can Help Us Grow*. (Penguin Random House LLC, New York. 2004-2005), p.48.

28   Wikipedia. "Imedi Media Holding," March 27, 2021. https://en.wikipedia.org/wiki/Imedi_Media_Holding

29   OWN. "Dr. Maya Angelou on Loving and Letting Go, Belief, Oprah Winfrey Network." *YouTube* video, 2:40. October 11, 2015. https://www.youtube.com/watch?v=7bTip3WGv2s

30   Paulo Coelho Blog. "Stories & Reflections," 2021. https://paulocoelhoblog.com/2007/12/10/the-lesson-of-the-butterfly/

31   Inspirationfeed. "80 Abraham-Hicks Quotes that will Make Your Life Flourish," March 6, 2021. https://inspirationfeed.com/abraham-hicks-quotes

OTHER WORKS OF RUSSO SHANIDZE

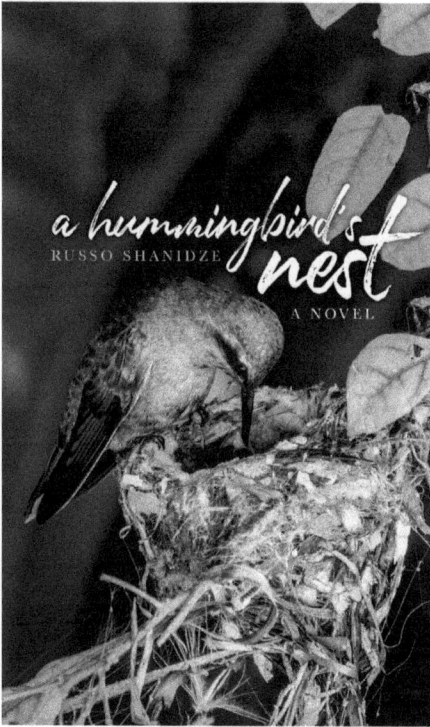

a hummingbird's nest
RUSSO SHANIDZE
A NOVEL

AUDIO POETRY BOOK

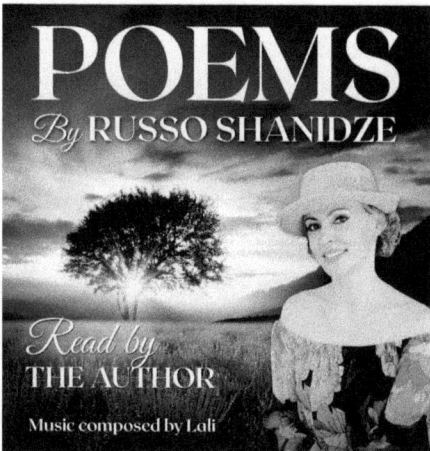

POEMS
By RUSSO SHANIDZE

Read by
THE AUTHOR

Music composed by Lali